GREAT MOMENTS IN
AMERICAN
AUTO RACING

GREAT MOMENTS IN AMERICAN AUTO RACING

By MATT CHRISTOPHER®
The #1 Sports Series for Kids

Bath Township
Library Center

LITTLE, BROWN AND COMPANY
NEW YORK • BOSTON

Little, Brown and Company

Hachette Book Group
237 Park Avenue, New York, NY 10017

Visit our website at www.lb-kids.com

www.mattchristopher.com

Little, Brown and Company is a division of Hachette Book Group, Inc.
The Little, Brown name and logo are trademarks of Hachette Book Group, Inc.

The publisher is not responsible for websites (or their content) that are not owned by the publisher.

First Edition: May 2011

Matt Christopher® is a registered trademark of Matt Christopher Royalties, Inc.

Text written by Stephanie True Peters

Library of Congress Cataloging-in-Publication Data

Christopher, Matt
Great moments in American auto racing / Matt Christopher
p. cm. — (The #1 sports series for kids)
ISBN 978-0-316-10297-1
1. Stock car racing—United States—History—Juvenile literature. 2. NASCAR (Association)—History—Juvenile literature. 3. Automobile racing—United States—History—Juvenile literature. I. Title.
GV1029.9.S74C48 2011
796.720973—dc22   2010041135

10 9 8 7 6 5 4 3 2 1

CWO

Printed in the United States of America

Contents

The Daytona 500

GREAT MOMENTS IN
AMERICAN
AUTO RACING

⋆ INTRODUCTION ⋆

Rev 'Em Up!

Have you ever dreamed of driving a car that can go more than two hundred miles per hour? If so, then you might be the next champion car racer. But what kind of car do you imagine yourself driving: open-wheeled or stock? Do you know the differences?

Open-wheeled race cars look very different from everyday cars. The wheels are set alongside the body of the car rather than below and are not covered by fenders. The chassis (the car's framework and body) rides low and has front and rear wings to help the car hug the pavement. These single-seaters offer little cover above the driver.

In the United States, these racers are called Indy cars. They get their name from the most famous race they enter—the Indianapolis 500. Every

Memorial Day weekend, hundreds of thousands of fans flock to the Indianapolis Motor Speedway in Indiana to watch the best Indy car drivers test their skills on the oval course.

Unlike Indy cars, stock cars look like regular cars. That's the only "regular" thing about them! These racers are made to take the beating of hundreds of fast-paced miles. Their engines are superpowered, and their chassis are built to minimize drag and maximize safety. Even the tires are different—they're filled with nitrogen, not air, so that they won't explode as they heat up on the track.

Stock car events in the United States are run by the National Association for Stock Car Auto Racing, or NASCAR. The highlight of NASCAR's year is the Daytona 500. Like its cousin in Indianapolis, the Daytona 500 attracts the finest drivers of its sport and fills the stands of the Daytona International Speedway with countless cheering fans.

These two races share many similarities. They're the same distance: 500 miles, or 200 laps. The Indy 500 is also known as "The Greatest Spectacle in Racing." The Daytona is called "The Great American Race." Each holds qualifying laps to determine which driver gets the best starting position, called the pole. Both races use a system of colored and patterned flags to tell the drivers when to go, slow down, or stop and when the race has been won. The races both start with a pace car leading the field once around the track so that the drivers can begin from a rolling, rather than a standing, start.

But not much else about these two events is the same. Thirty-three cars participate in the Indy 500; 43 race in the Daytona 500. The Indy 500 takes place on Memorial Day every May; leading up to the race is Festival 500, a month of activities that celebrate cars and past races. The Daytona 500 is in mid-February after Speed Weeks, a two-week-long NASCAR extravaganza that includes sports cars and truck racing plus two days of qualifiers. Daytona drivers are typically from the United States, while the field of Indy drivers is more international.

Now, maybe you already count yourself as a fan of car racing. But if you want to know even more about the most exciting moments of the Indianapolis 500 and the Daytona 500, then put on your seat belt, rev your engine—and speed into the pages of this book!

THE INDIANAPOLIS 500

★ CHAPTER ONE ★

1909–1921

The Brickyard

Carl Fisher, owner of a car headlight company, had an idea. He wanted people to come to his hometown, Indianapolis, Indiana, to buy cars. If they did, then he'd sell more headlights.

But how could he get people to come? That was the big question.

The answer, Fisher believed, lay in car racing. Car racing had been around almost as long as cars themselves. The first gasoline-powered car was built sometime between 1885 and 1886 by German manufacturer Karl Friedrich Benz. The first race took place on June 22, 1894, when 21 cars drove for first place from Paris to Rouen in France. A year later, the United States held its first race, a round-trip journey in Illinois from Chicago to Evanston and back.

Hundreds of car enthusiasts followed these and later events closely, either in person or through newspaper accounts. By the early 1900s, car racing had become a very popular sport, generating huge crowds of rabid fans. Fisher wanted to bring that fan base to Indianapolis. So in 1904, he decided to build a state-of-the-art racetrack there.

The Indianapolis Motor Speedway, a two-and-a-half-mile oval with four banked corners and a surface of tar covered with crushed stone, opened three years later. On August 19, 1909, the track held one of its first events, a 300-mile race.

It was a disaster.

As the race progressed, the track disintegrated. The asphalt melted under the hot sun. The crushed-stone surface became unstable. One car skidded off the track and flipped, killing the driver and his riding mechanic. Another mechanic and two spectators died later when a blown tire sent a car lunging into the stands. When yet another accident occurred, officials canceled the remaining laps and closed the track.

Fisher knew he had to do something to save his Speedway. Since the surface was the problem, he repaved the oval with 3.2 million bricks.

"The Brickyard," as the Speedway was now nick-named, held three small events in 1910. In 1911, Fisher focused on one spectacular 500-mile race. The distance was determined by the number of hours (seven) he guessed spectators would watch cars race multiplied by the cars' top speed (seventy-five miles per hour). He chose May 30, Memorial Day, for the first Indianapolis 500-Mile International Sweepstakes.

Forty drivers entered the event. One was Ray Harroun, who sat behind the wheel of the Wasp, the only single-seater in the race. Back then, there were two men in every race car—the driver and the riding mechanic, who helped keep the car going and warned the driver of approaching cars.

Instead of a riding mechanic, Harroun had the first-ever rearview mirror, which he invented. It didn't work very well.

"The thing vibrated so much I couldn't see out of it," he admitted.

The resurfaced track was a big improvement, and the cars chewed up the course. By mile 300, Harroun and Ralph Mulford had left the others behind. Then Harroun was stopped with a blown tire. When he entered his pit (an offtrack area where cars stop to refuel and be repaired), Mulford roared past—and then hit the pits with his own tire troubles!

While Mulford pitted, Harroun recaptured the lead. After six hours, forty-two minutes, and eight seconds, he crossed the finish line to become the first winner of the Indy 500.

But had he really won? Mulford argued that he had lapped Harroun during Harroun's tire change. Therefore, he was the winner, not Harroun.

His protests fell on deaf ears. Mulford accepted the verdict with grace—although he always believed that he was the true victor.

Just 24 cars lined up for the second Indy 500. Among them was the Gray Ghost, a Mercedes driven by dirt-track champion Ralph DePalma. With his riding mechanic Rupert Jeffkins at his side—a rule change now required a second man in every car—DePalma sped to the front, where he stayed for the next 194 laps!

Then, in lap 197, the Ghost began to backfire. With less than a mile to go, it quit altogether. DePalma and Jeffkins refused to give up. They jumped out and pushed the Mercedes across the finish line!

Their heroic efforts didn't count for anything, though. The rules stated that cars had to cross the line under their own power. Joe Dawson was declared the victor after having led for only two laps—the least number of any Indy 500 winner ever.

The next two Indys were won by Frenchmen, first Jules Goux and then René Thomas. In 1915, DePalma took the lead when, in a bizarre repeat of the 1912 race, his Mercedes began to buck with just three laps remaining. Luckily, the car finished without help, earning DePalma his only Brickyard victory.

The 1916 race was unusual because its distance was shortened to 300 miles. World War I was raging throughout Europe, and while the United States had yet to enter the conflict, the country had little time or money for racing. The victor, Dario Resta, is the only driver to win the Indy "300."

In April 1917, the United States declared war on Germany. The track closed until 1918, when the international conflict ended.

The first postwar Indy 500 was won by Howard "Howdy" Wilcox of Indianapolis with a track record average speed of 88.05 miles per hour. That same day, René Thomas reached the fastest speed ever in the race, 104.8 miles per hour. Sadly, their accomplishments were overshadowed by the deaths of drivers Arthur Thurman and Louis LeCocq, whose accidents were caused by the increased speeds. A mechanic was also killed in the explosion that engulfed LeCocq's car; another was badly injured but survived.

In 1920, Ralph DePalma nearly made history as the first driver to win twice at the Brickyard. He was in the lead when his engine burst into flames. DePalma continued to drive while his mechanic (and nephew), Pete DePaolo, crawled onto the hood and put out the flames.

Meanwhile, Gaston Chevrolet roared into the lead. He had almost run out of gas, but a quick fuel stop solved the problem, allowing Chevrolet to cross the finish line in first place.

Tragically, seven months later, Chevrolet was killed in a racing accident in California. Tommy Milton, the driver hired by Arthur and Louis Chevrolet to take their brother Gaston's place, won the Indy 500 the following year—an amazing achievement considering he was nearly blind!

★ CHAPTER TWO ★

1922–1933

"That's a Duesey!"

In 10 years, the average speed at the Brickyard had risen from 75 to 90 miles per hour. In 1922, that number jumped to 95. The winning car, driven by Jimmy Murphy, was designed by brothers August and Fred Duesenberg.

Innovative designs make good race cars—and, as Tommy Milton discovered, innovation sometimes keeps good cars running. He was tearing up the oval in 1923 when his gas-tank cap fell off. His pit crew didn't have a replacement, so someone wrapped an orange with thick tape and shoved it into the tank opening! Milton zoomed over the finish line—and into the history books as the first driver to win two Indianapolis 500s.

"Two" was the number of drivers it took to win

the 1924 race. Lora L. Corum and Joe Boyer were each driving Duesenberg cars. Boyer was running well ahead of the pack until engine trouble knocked his car out of the race.

Meanwhile, the more cautious Corum stayed in the middle. That upset Fred Duesenberg. When Corum pulled off to pit in lap 109, Duesenberg ordered him out of the car—and put Boyer back in the race in Corum's place!

"Put it in front or burn it up," Duesenberg instructed Boyer. Boyer obeyed, speeding from behind to victory. Because Corum had driven for half the race, however, he shared the win with Boyer.

Pete DePaolo was at the helm of a Duesenberg the next year. His uncle, Ralph DePalma, was also on the track. Neither was thinking about the other when the green flag waved; they were thinking about speed!

And at the 1925 Indy 500, speed was king. DePaolo and two other drivers surpassed the 100-mile-per-hour mark.

DePaolo was near the lead throughout the first half. It took great effort to stay there; his hands became badly blistered from the steering wheel and needed medical attention. So Duesenberg replaced him temporarily.

"My heart ached to see my baby rolling away from the pits without me," DePaolo recalled.

Once behind the wheel again, DePaolo streaked into the lead and crossed the finish line at 4:56:39, the fastest time ever. His average speed of 101.127 was also a track record that stood for the next seven years.

As for Uncle Ralph, he finished seventh in his final Indy 500. DePalma continued racing until his retirement in 1934. By his own reckoning, he had won 2,257 races out of 2,889 entered, making him one of the most successful drivers of all time.

In 1926, fate put relief driver Frank Lockhart behind the wheel for the Indy 500. He might have watched from the pits had fellow driver Peter Kreis not come down with the flu. From his hospital bed, Kreis instructed his crew to "put the kid in the car"—meaning 23-year-old Lockhart.

Midway through the race, fate smiled on Lockhart a second time. He was battling against Harry Hartz for first. Then Hartz pulled into the pit. To his horror, his car wouldn't restart! As the crew frantically worked the crank, Hartz realized he hadn't turned on the ignition.

Hartz's mistake gave Lockhart the extra seconds he needed. When the race was called in lap 160 on account of rain, he became the youngest driver to win the Indy 500, an honor he held for the next 26 years.

Lockhart was driving to win the next year when a connecting rod on his car broke. Indiana native and first-time Indy 500 racer George Souders guided his Duesenberg in and around the competition to finish a full 12 minutes ahead of the runner-up.

Souders's victory marked the last time a "Duesey" won the Indy 500. It also marked the end of Carl Fisher's ownership of the Speedway. Fisher had been looking to sell the Brickyard since 1923. Now he found a buyer in Eddie Rickenbacker, a famous World War I flying ace.

Rickenbacker was no stranger to the Speedway. Before going to war in 1917, he competed in four Indy 500s. While he never finished higher than 10th place, he had a soft spot for the Brickyard.

The Rickenbacker era started off with a bang with a duel in 1928 between two rookies named Lou in the last lap. Lou Meyer gunned across for the checkered flag 44 seconds before runner-up Lou Moore.

Tragedy hit the racing world after that race. In November, Indy 500 veterans Norman Batten and Earl DeVore were lost at sea during a vacation. At the 1929 Indy, Bill Spence flipped during a turn and rolled several times before stopping. He died of his injuries. Ray Keech won the event that year—but two weeks later, he was killed in a racing accident in Pennsylvania.

The 1930 Indy 500 was held during the Great Depression, a time of terrible economic woes. Few drivers had money for new cars, so they used spare parts to build racers or drove older models.

Sadly, these older cars led to another fatality. Rickenbacker had insisted on riding mechanics in each car. One of these men, Paul Marshall, died when the car driven by his brother Cy crashed.

The next Memorial Day race was another crash-filled horror show. A few drivers were seriously injured; 11-year-old Wilbur Brink paid the ultimate price. Wilbur was playing in his front yard near the Speedway when a wheel flew out of the course and hit him, killing him.

The 1932 Indy saw Fred Frame surpass Pete

DePaolo's longtime speed record with an average of 104.144 miles per hour. Frame's record lasted only until the next year, however, when Lou Meyer won his second Indy with a speed of 104.162. Three drivers and two mechanics lost their lives that day.

And yet, even with the deaths, accidents, and injuries, the Indianapolis 500 continued on its path to becoming one of the most popular events in car racing.

⋆ CHAPTER THREE ⋆

1934–1941

Racing Speeds Up – and Then Stops

After the deaths in 1933, many hoped drivers of the Indy 500 would slow down for safety's sake. But the 100-plus-mile-per-hour speeds that had once seemed unattainable were now the norm. Turning back the clock to a slower era proved impossible.

In fact, the average winning speed steadily increased, from 104.863 in 1934 (winner: Bill Cummings) to 106.240 in 1935 (winner: Kelly Petillo) and to 109.069 in 1936 (winner: Lou Meyer). Then, in 1937, it blew past the 110-mile-per-hour mark completely to hit 113.580!

The winner that year was Wilbur Shaw. "When the starting flag goes down, you become an integral part of a tornado," Shaw once said of racing, "and there's nothing you can do but pray."

Shaw led the "tornado" for 131 of the 200 laps during the 1937 race. With just 20 laps remaining, victory seemed certain. Then trouble struck. His car began to lose oil—not a good thing for an engine. In addition, one of his tires was wearing out. The combination forced him to slow his pace.

That gave Ralph Hepburn the chance he'd been waiting for. He shot forward, gradually closing the gap between them.

With the finish line ahead and Hepburn gaining on him from behind, Shaw gunned his engine, praying it would hold out. In the final stretch, the two cars were almost side by side. Then— *vroom!*—Shaw streaked over the line 2.16 seconds before Hepburn!

The next year, Shaw came in second after being lapped twice by Floyd Roberts. Sadly, Roberts was killed at the Brickyard a year later while trying to avoid a multicar accident.

That 1939 race was almost the end of three-time Indy winner Lou Meyer, too. Meyer wasn't seeking a fourth crown, just a safe finish.

With just 40 miles to go, he blew a tire and careened toward the wall. He returned to the track only to spin out into the wall again. He eventually finished, but he retired soon afterward. Apparently, he'd had enough near misses to suit him!

Shaw captured his second Indy crown that same day. Then, in 1940, he tied Meyer with a third victory at the Speedway. Rain slowed the drivers to 75 miles per hour for the final 125 miles. It may not have been an exciting finish for anyone but Shaw, the first driver to win back-to-back races at the Speedway.

There was plenty of excitement for the 1941 Indy 500, especially for Shaw. The day before the race, he inspected his car. One of the tires looked faulty, so he removed it, marked it with chalk to be used as a spare, and set it aside in the pits. That taken care of, he didn't give the matter another thought.

He certainly wasn't thinking about the tire the next morning. Instead, he was thinking about his car, which was nearly consumed by an enormous fire near the track garages! Thanks to water from the firefighters' hoses, his car was saved.

What he didn't know was that the same water

washed off his chalk mark. Now the faulty tire looked the same as all the others.

When the race began, Shaw left all but two other drivers, Mauri Rose and Rex Mays, behind. Then, in lap 40, Rose was sidelined with spark plug problems. That didn't sit well with the car's owner, Lou Moore. Moore had another vehicle in the race, but that car's driver, Floyd Davis, didn't have Rose's skill. Moore replaced him with Rose.

Rose quickly gained on Mays and passed him. He drew close to Shaw, too, but Shaw didn't give up his lead easily. In fact, he wouldn't have given it up at all if not for the faulty tire.

That tire was no longer in the pits. It was on his car. In lap 152, it gave out. Shaw spun into the wall. His fuel tank burst, showering everything in gasoline.

Had that gasoline ignited, Shaw's life could have ended in a fireball. As it was, he couldn't move from the waist down, for his back had been injured, leaving him temporarily paralyzed. Fortunately, the emergency crew came to the rescue and he survived.

Meanwhile, Rose crossed the finish line in Davis's car. The two were declared co-winners of the race, the second and last time two drivers would share the crown.

Wilbur Shaw's driving career ended that day in 1941, but not because of his accident. Once again, the major world powers were at war. When the Japanese bombed Pearl Harbor shortly after Memorial Day, the United States entered World War II.

The Indianapolis Motor Speedway shuttered its gates for four long years while the war raged overseas. Only after Adolf Hitler and his Nazi regime were defeated did the engines rev again at the Brickyard.

Those years had not been kind to the track. Weeds grew through the bricks. The buildings were falling apart. The grandstands and bleachers sagged.

When Wilbur Shaw saw the track, he was stunned by its condition—and saddened by the news that Eddie Rickenbacker had put it up for sale. Rumors swirled that the property would be turned into a housing development. In a last-ditch effort to preserve the track, Shaw persuaded successful Indiana businessman Anton "Tony" Hulman to buy it. Together, they refurbished the oval—and a new era at the Speedway began.

★ CHAPTER FOUR ★

1946–1950

Holland vs. Rose

After sitting dormant for four years, the Brickyard reopened for the 1946 Indianapolis 500. It was in great shape thanks to Shaw and Hulman. Unfortunately, the cars that showed up for the qualifying runs weren't. Most were hand-me-downs from previous races, some from as long ago as the 1930s. Still, the 33 available spots filled quickly.

In the lineup were George Robson and Jimmy Jackson. Robson was a relative newcomer to the Speedway, having made just two trips before World War II. Jackson was even newer; 1946 was his first Indy 500. He made headlines instantly because of the car he was driving. It wasn't the model or the engine design that grabbed attention, but the fact that it was painted green.

Like most sports, car racing has its share of rituals and superstitions. The most famous ritual of the Indy 500 is the drinking of milk in Victory Lane. This tradition started in 1936, when Lou Meyer was photographed drinking buttermilk after his win. Ever since then, the winners have guzzled milk in Victory Lane.

As for green cars, that superstition started in 1920 with Gaston Chevrolet. That year, he drove a green car to victory at the Speedway. Months later, however, he lost control of that same green car and was killed. From then on, green cars were shunned at the Indy 500 and most other racetracks.

When Jackson appeared behind the wheel of a green car, dire predictions about his fate hummed through the Speedway. But as the race began, the powerful roar from Jackson's car drowned out those hums. In fact, his auto did what only eight others did that day—finish the race!

Unfortunately for Jackson, he didn't finish in first place. That prize went to George Robson, who took command of the field early on and held it to claim the biggest Indy 500 purse—more than forty-two thousand dollars—yet.

Sadly, Robson perished in early September in a

racing accident in Georgia. Jackson competed five more times but never finished higher than fifth place.

The following year, fans were electrified by one of the greatest Indy 500 rivalries of all time. Mauri Rose had shared a trip to Victory Lane years before. Bill Holland was a talented rookie. Both were in cars designed by former Indy great Lou Moore. Moore himself was in the pits to watch his cars perform.

Holland may have been new to the race, but he drove like a veteran. Going into the final laps, he was in first place with Rose in second. As Holland roared past his pit, Moore had the crew hold up a chalkboard with the letters *EZY* on it. The meaning of the message was clear—Holland was to ease up in the final miles.

Holland, believing that the message also meant that he had a comfortable lead over Rose, obeyed Moore's command. As he slowed, Rose sped up and passed him. The two exchanged waves. Holland thought Rose was congratulating him.

But what Holland didn't realize was that Rose was now in first place. Rose wasn't waving to say "Good job!" but "See you later!"

How did Rose know he now had the lead? Simple: Moore had told him via the message *P 1* on the chalkboard. Moore purposefully hid that message from Holland. He didn't want his rookie driver to put his car in jeopardy by racing it full out in the last laps.

Rose zoomed to victory with Holland close behind. In fact, Holland believed he had won and was shocked to learn that he had placed second. "I figured I was still laps in front," he said later, shaking his head in anger at Moore's chalkboard maneuver.

Holland came close to finishing first the next year but again wound up watching Rose's back fender streak over the finish line before him. There was no doubt this time that Rose had won, for both drivers had put the pedal to the metal in their efforts to take first.

Holland finally had his day at the races in 1949. He had a captive audience for his victory, too, and not just the spectators in the stands. For the first time ever, the Indy 500 was broadcast on television. Local station WFBM recorded every lap of what initially looked to be yet another one-two Rose-Holland finish.

But this year, Rose's car broke down. Holland,

with an average speed of 121.327, cruised unchallenged to take the checkered flag. Holland beat Rose again in 1950, although they were second and third that year, not first and second. The victor then was Johnnie Parsons, a skilled driver who had placed second the year before.

Still, some speculate that Parsons might not have won if the weather hadn't helped him. Rose and Holland were creeping up on him when the track was suddenly swamped by a torrential downpour. Conditions were too harrowing for the race to continue; it ended in lap 138 with Parsons as the winner.

Unfortunately for Indy 500 fans, that year was the last of the Holland-Rose rivalry. Rose drove the race in 1951 but came close to being killed in an accident caused by a wheel malfunction. He managed to walk away from the crash and retired soon after.

Holland, on the other hand, didn't compete in either the 1951 or 1952 Indy 500. Back then, the track's governing body, the American Automobile Association (AAA), didn't allow Indy car drivers to race in events run by NASCAR. This rule was later reversed, but when Holland ignored it in late 1951, he was suspended for a year. He returned to the oval in Indianapolis one last time in 1953, where he placed a disappointing 15th.

Race car fans may not have been paying all that much attention to Holland by then, however, for a new driver named Bill Vukovich had roared onto the scene and stolen the show.

★ CHAPTER FIVE ★

1951–1955

Vukovich

"The only way to win here," legendary driver Bill Vukovich once said of racing at the Brickyard, "is to keep your foot on the throttle and turn left."

Vukovich was a champion midget car racer. Midget cars are small but powerful open-wheeled vehicles. In 1951, he made the jump from midgets to the Indy 500. He lasted just 29 laps before his car suffered an oil tank problem. Still, his driving caught the attention of owner Howard Keck.

Keck hired Vukovich to drive for him in the 1952 Indy 500. Vukovich combined skill and daring to lead the field for 150 of the 200 laps. The win looked in the bag when, just eight laps from the finish, something went wrong with his steering. Vukovich was forced to pull over. Twenty-two-year-old Troy Ruttman roared past him and into Victory Lane—and into the record books as the youngest driver yet to win the Indy 500.

Many hoped Ruttman and Vukovich would be the next great rivals of the Brickyard. But it was not to be. Months after winning the 500, Ruttman broke his arm in another race. He returned to the track in 1954, but his driving skills had gone downhill.

Vukovich, on the other hand, fulfilled every 500 fan's dream in his third try at the crown.

The weather in Indianapolis in late May can be very unpredictable. Sudden drenching rains had shut or slowed the track many times. In 1953, it wasn't rain that caused problems but sun. The day started out as a scorcher and just got hotter. One driver, Carl Scarborough, even died because of the heat that day.

Vukovich, however, looked cool as a cucumber behind the wheel. He started in the coveted pole position. When the race began, he completely dominated the field. Mile after mile, lap after lap, it was Vukovich first and everyone else behind him. He crossed the finish line after driving without relief for nearly four hours at a speed of 128.740

miles per hour. In all, he led for an astonishing 195 out of 200 laps, the second-best showing in Indy 500 history.

Vukovich was the name on everyone's lips the next Memorial Day. But it wasn't his driving prowess that had them talking; it was the fact that he had barely qualified! His driving wasn't to blame, however. His car was plagued with problems that were finally fixed in time for him to take the 19th start position.

Ahead of him was pole winner John James "Jack" McGrath, who had broken the speed-trial record with a speed of 141.003 miles per hour. Also there were Jimmy Daywalt and Jimmy Bryan. All hoped that Vukovich's poor showing in the qualifiers would give them a better chance to win.

Bryan's hopes undoubtedly grew stronger soon after the race began. He took the lead early on and then played a game of tag with McGrath and Daywalt. Daywalt lasted more than half the race before an accident in lap 111 knocked him out.

Meanwhile, Vukovich was keeping a very careful eye on the leaders. Near the midway mile mark, he noticed that McGrath, now in second behind Bryan, appeared to be tiring. Slowly, he picked his way through the pack until he drew alongside McGrath. Then, with one smooth move, he passed him!

That left Bryan in Vukovich's way, but not for long. Bryan had been riding his car hard all day. Now, just when Bryan needed his vehicle to perform its best, it began to deteriorate. Shock absorbers, brakes, an oil leak—one thing after another went wrong.

Vukovich sensed weakness. Like a shark circling its prey, he moved in. At mile 375, he passed Bryan. He held that lead, and when the checkered flag flew, he had his second Indy 500 crown!

Vukovich was the third driver after Wilbur Shaw and Mauri Rose to win back-to-back 500s. But he had done something they hadn't: shatter the race's existing average speed record. His 130.840 miles per hour topped Ruttman's 128.922 from 1952. Bryan managed to keep his car together to take second, with McGrath placing third.

After such an amazing performance, everyone expected Vukovich's run at a third Indy victory to be unforgettable. It was, but for the worst possible reason.

Despite starting in the fifth position, Vukovich was predicted to win the 1955 Indy 500. After 56 laps, it seemed those predictions would come true. That all changed at turn 2 of the 57th lap, when chaos broke loose.

Driver Johnny Boyd was right there on the track when it happened. He saw the axle on fellow racer Rodger Ward's car break as Ward entered turn 2. "I saw Ward swerve, hit the inside wall, and flip," he recalled.

Boyd did his best to avoid Ward, only to be hit by another driver, Al Keller. Boyd's car tumbled upside down and landed right in Vukovich's path. "It felt like a freight train running over me," Boyd recalled of the moment Vukovich's car plowed into him.

Boyd was unhurt in the crash. Vukovich was not so fortunate. A video clip shows Vukovich's car flipping over the outside rail, bouncing high into the air, and somersaulting end over end several times before finally coming to rest.

"I think I'd be short when I say he flipped 20 to 25 feet into the air," a Speedway historian later reported. "He was almost as high up as the trees."

Ed Elisian hit the brakes, leaped out of his car, and rushed across the track to the wreck. But by the time he reached him, Vukovich was dead.

"Bill Vukovich was probably the greatest actual

driver we have ever known in terms of his skill and his determination," Rodger Ward once said. With his death, the sports world mourned the loss of yet another of its most accomplished racers and colorful personalities.

★ CHAPTER SIX ★
1956–1960

"Down to the Cord"

Race car drivers can get seriously injured or even killed while engaged in the sport they love. Knowing this, track owners, car owners, drivers, and the sports' governing body are always on the alert for ways to improve safety.

Unfortunately, sometimes those improvements come after tragedies occur, not before. In 1958, Pat O'Connor was crushed when his car flipped over on top of him. Very soon afterward, roll bars were required on all race cars. In 1959, Jerry Unser, the eldest of three race car brothers, died of burns during a pre–Indy 500 practice run. His death made fire-resistant suits mandatory for all drivers.

Fans at the Brickyard saw new faces enter Victory Lane in the second half of the 1950s. Pat Flaherty, a veteran of three other Indys, survived a track littered with crashes and slick with rain to take the crown in 1956. Sam Hanks proved that number 13 can be lucky when he finally won in 1957, his 13th attempt.

The 1958 Indy 500 introduced the world to eight new drivers, including future superstar A. J. Foyt Jr. Foyt finished 16th behind winner Jimmy Bryan, yet his raw talent was obvious to anyone who saw him at the wheel.

The 1959 Indy was overshadowed by the deaths of Jerry Unser and Bob Cortner, who crashed into the outside wall during a qualifier. Tony Bettenhausen might have added his name to the list of fatalities, too, if not for the roll bar. Instead, he walked away from his crash relatively unharmed to place fourth that year behind winner Rodger Ward.

That Ward had completed the race, let alone won, was somewhat miraculous. A postrace inspection of his car showed that the piston plug was broken. If he'd had to drive much longer, he would have fallen far behind runner-up Jim Rathmann. Instead, he won by 23 seconds.

Rathmann must have been looking to even things up at the 1960 Indy 500. Of course, Ward was just as eager to defend his title. This led to one of the greatest driving duels of the Brickyard's history.

Ward jumped to an early lead only to see his advantage slip away during a one-minute pit stop in lap 43. One minute may not seem that long, but Rathmann's pit took only 31 seconds. When cars are moving at upward of 135 miles per hour, 29 seconds is plenty of time to take a commanding lead!

Ward and Rathmann pitted again in the 86th lap. Rathmann was still ahead by half a minute. If Ward was to overtake him, he had to be in and out of the pits faster than Rathmann.

He was. Rathmann needed 21 seconds. Ward took only 15. Rathmann was still ahead—but Ward wasn't so far behind anymore.

As the miles passed beneath their tires, Ward edged closer to Rathmann. At the 100-lap mark, he was 14 seconds behind. Twenty laps later, he was breathing down Rathmann's neck.

That was the start of an unbelievable showdown. Ward overtook Rathmann in lap 123. He held the lead until lap 127, when Rathmann streaked past him. In lap 142, Ward zoomed by to recover the front spot.

Back and forth the two went. Ward was in the

lead in lap 194, but Rathmann remained close behind. The fans in the stands were going wild trying to guess who would come out the victor!

But on the track, Ward knew that Rathmann had the race. "I wasn't thinking that tires were going to be that serious of a problem," he remembered years later.

They were problematic. Ward had been pushing his car so hard that one of his tires had almost completely worn out. If he tried to outrun Rathmann in the final laps, that tire would undoubtedly fail. Ward wasn't willing to risk it.

In lap 197, Rathmann, a three-time Indy 500 runner-up, passed Ward one last time. He crossed the finish line 12.67 seconds before Ward. His average speed of 138.767 miles per hour was a track record. The funny thing was, the trouble that had caused Ward to slow down had nearly been a problem for Rathmann's car, too.

"In Victory Circle, if you looked at his own right rear [tire], it was down to the cord," Ward said. "It just got there after mine did."

Rathmann and Ward were one and two that year. Far behind them was A. J. Foyt Jr.

Foyt was just eight years old when he drove a

midget racer out of his father's garage—and into the side of his house. Fortunately, he was unharmed and just as in love with driving as ever. As a teenager, he raced on dirt tracks. Then in 1958, at age 23, he got his first crack at the Indy 500.

"That race morning, I was a nervous wreck," Foyt admitted, "saying 'Is this what I want to do for a living or not?' "

The answer to that question was a resounding yes. He finished 16th that day and entered again in 1959 and 1960, placing 10th and 25th. If one looked at just those finishes, it might seem that Foyt was not that skilled a driver. But outside of Indianapolis, he was tearing up courses throughout the country. In 1960 alone, he won his first national Indy car championship and the eastern division of the United States Auto Club (USAC) sprint car championship, came in second in the California midget circuit, and came in third in the Midwest Sprints.

In short, Foyt wasn't just good—he was great, as he proved to everyone the next year.

★ CHAPTER SEVEN ★

1961–1965

New Faces, Faster Races

Memorial Day 1961 marked the 45th running of the Indy 500. Jim Hurtubise surged into an early lead that day. Thirty-five laps later, Jim Rathmann swept by him, only to be passed himself by rookie Parnelli Jones. Jones gave up his advantage two laps later to Eddie Sachs but recovered it in lap 52 and held it for the next 23 laps.

Meanwhile, A. J. Foyt Jr. was moving through the field. He stole Jones's first-place slot in lap 76 but then lost it to hard-running Troy Ruttman. The two traded places four times until Ruttman's clutch broke, sending him to the sidelines for good.

Now Foyt had to deal with Eddie Sachs. In a duel as thrilling as the one between Rathmann and Ward, Foyt and Sachs swapped the first- and second-place spots. Foyt had the lead when, suddenly, his engine bucked. He pulled into the pits in lap 184, where he learned that his fuel tank was almost empty!

Foyt was confused—hadn't his crew refueled the car on his last stop? The problem, it turned out, was a faulty gas nozzle. The nozzle was replaced, the tank was filled, and Foyt was back in business.

Unfortunately for Foyt, Sachs now had a 30-second lead. Foyt's quest for victory seemed impossible—until Sachs veered off to fix a bad tire.

With just three laps to go, Foyt gunned the engine. He flashed past Sachs moments before Sachs left the pits. He held the lead for the remaining two laps, and when the checkered flag flew, Foyt was the winner!

Foyt had hoped to duplicate Shaw's and Vukovich's back-to-back triumphs the next year, but it was not to be. On the 69th lap, he lost a wheel. Ward fared better, taking his second 500 with a track-best speed of 140.293.

In 1963, Parnelli Jones coasted into Victory Lane, although his win was controversial. Jones had the lead when his engine started to smoke. But instead of fixing his car's problem, Jones drove it to the checkered flag.

That didn't sit well with Eddie Sachs, who claimed his car had skidded out on oil leaked from Jones's car. He later told Jones he hadn't deserved to win. Jones reacted by punching Sachs in the nose!

The 1964 Indy saw Jones and Sachs together in the lineup again, along with Foyt, Ward, Johnny Boyd, and other familiar faces. Also there was rookie Dave MacDonald.

MacDonald usually raced stock cars. In early 1964, he was offered the chance to drive in the Indy 500, in a car designed to carry enough fuel to last the entire race. Other drivers had refused, saying that the car handled badly. MacDonald accepted.

That would prove to be a fatal decision.

In the second lap, MacDonald passed Johnny Rutherford. Rutherford noticed that MacDonald's car was moving strangely. "Whoa," he recalled thinking. "He's either going to win this thing or crash."

Moments later, MacDonald lost control. The car slammed into the wall and exploded. Eddie Sachs plowed into MacDonald. His car, like MacDonald's, had a full tank of gasoline; like MacDonald's car, it burst into flames. Emergency vehicles rushed to the scene, but it was too late. Both Sachs and MacDonald died.

After the fiery collision, gasoline was banned in favor of safer, alcohol-based fuel; fuel tanks were redesigned to resist punctures and cracks.

In 1965, a charismatic new driver joined the lineup. Mario Andretti was born in Italy but had lived in Nazareth, Pennsylvania, since 1955. Nazareth had a half-mile dirt racetrack, and it was there that Andretti got his start.

"I don't remember as a kid wanting to do or be anything else but…a race driver," Andretti remembered.

In 1960 and 1961, Andretti entered 46 stock car races—and won an amazing 21. As successful as he was there, he wanted to drive single-seaters.

With that goal in mind, he switched to midget cars. In 1963, while driving a victory lap after his third win in three races, he heard words that sounded like music to his ears.

"Mario," the track announcer boomed over the loudspeaker, "with this feature win, it looks to me like you just bought a ticket to the big time."

Two years later, the announcer's prediction came true: Mario Andretti was in the Indy 500, starting out in the number-four spot.

Scotsman Jim Clark had also qualified. Clark had

come in second behind Parnelli Jones two years earlier. In 1964, he was in the lead when his car broke down. Now he was ready to get the job done when the green flag flew.

Foyt was just as ready. From almost the first lap, he and Clark revved ahead of the field. First Foyt led, then Clark, with Andretti and Jones trailing not far behind. Foyt surged to the lead during Clark's pit stop in lap 67 but fell behind eight laps later when he ran out of fuel before reaching his pits. Clark screamed past while Foyt fumed.

Foyt jumped back into second when he reentered the race, but in lap 116, his transmission gave out. That was it for him that day.

By that time, Clark was so far ahead that no one could catch him. His top speed was just over 150 miles per hour, a track record and more than fast enough for him to hold a two-lap lead—and to coast to victory at a throttled-back 140 miles per hour.

"I'll admit I expected a more competitive race," Clark quipped.

Mario Andretti, meanwhile, came in third after Parnelli Jones. When he crossed the line, he was already looking forward to the next year.

★ CHAPTER EIGHT ★

1966–1971

"Fantastic, Confused, and Incredible"

Jim Clark was only one of two non-Americans in the 1965 Indy 500. In 1966 that number doubled, with three drivers hailing from Great Britain and one from Canada. The British invaded Victory Lane as well as the lineup—although at least one newspaper claimed winner Graham Hill owed his success to the problems of others.

"He never passed a car all day long," the *Indianapolis Star* reported.

The problems started with a disastrous 16-car pileup before one lap was even run. That tangle, and another that followed almost immediately after, eliminated Foyt and other favorites from contention. Pack leader Andretti joined them on the sidelines later when his car blew a valve. British race star Jackie Stewart nearly had it won when his car stalled, the victim of a sudden oil leak.

The *Star* described the race as "the most fantastic, confused, and incredible 500."

Incredible was the word for the finish of the 1967 Indy 500. The field thinned out early on, with Andretti departing after losing a tire and Clark and Hill leaving with burned pistons. Jones and Foyt battled for supremacy for much of the remainder of the race. Then, with less than 10 miles remaining, Jones was forced to his pit with a broken transmission.

That left Foyt. He was coming into the front straightaway of his final lap when—*wham!*—five cars wrecked right in front of him!

"I couldn't believe my eyes," he recalled. "I dropped it into second gear and decided that if I hit anyone, I was going to push them across the start-finish line."

Luckily for everyone, Foyt threaded his car through the mess to cross the line at just 50 miles per hour for his third Indy 500 win.

The history of Indianapolis 500 is full of such heart-stopping crashes, miraculous photo finishes, and lively personalities. There are also several stories of drivers who almost won but didn't. Of those men, Lloyd Ruby stands out as the man who came closest the most often.

Ruby had been in every Indy since 1960. In 1964, he drove his best race yet, coming in third after Foyt and Ward. Many fans believed he was finally on the verge of breaking through. But in 1965, a blown engine forced him out of the race. That was the first incident in what has to be one of the longest strings of bad luck in racing history.

In 1966, Ruby was leading the charge for 68 laps when a cam stud broke. A year later, he had gone less than three miles when he suffered valve troubles. He managed to complete the entire race in 1968 and even led for 42 laps before dropping behind to fifth place.

In 1969, he had the lead when he pitted to refuel. His tank full, he got the go-ahead to rejoin the race. He hadn't moved more than three feet when he heard the sound of metal tearing. The fuel nozzle was still stuck in the tank! Fuel gushed out of a gaping hole, flooding the pits, the car, and the nearby crew.

"We could make pit stops all day long and something like this would never happen again," Ruby said. "When they told me to get out of the car, I couldn't believe it."

While Ruby was staring dumbfounded at his fuel-soaked car, Andretti, Foyt, and veteran driver Dan Gurney were fighting for first place. Andretti, like Ruby, had been plagued by car problems at the Indy 500 for years. Now, however, he had the lead, and when Foyt was forced to drop out with an overheated engine, his chances improved even more. Gurney tried his best to overtake Andretti, but he couldn't. Andretti crossed the finish line with a record-breaking time of 3:11:14 as well as the race's fastest average speed of 156.867 miles per hour.

"I prayed those last 150 miles," a joyful but exhausted Andretti told reporters. "So many things have happened to me here in the past."

Those "things" included a lost wheel in 1967 and piston trouble in 1968, and unfortunately, more of those "things" awaited him in future races. He placed sixth in 1970 but a year later crashed in turn 3 after completing just 11 laps. And in 1972, he ran out of fuel at 15 miles from the finish!

Lloyd Ruby's bad-luck streak continued into the new decade. An oil leak followed by an engine fire forced him out of the 1970 Indy. In 1971, gear trouble sidelined him. In the next trip to the Brickyard, he lasted for all but four laps before being flagged to the pits.

The same year that gear trouble ruined Ruby's chances and Andretti crashed in turn 3, Al Unser earned his second Indianapolis 500 crown. That put him in the record books alongside Wilbur Shaw, Mauri Rose, and Bill Vukovich as one of four drivers to win back-to-back Indys.

His 1970 triumph was the second time someone with the name Unser drove into Victory Lane. His brother Bobby had won the Indy in 1968. With Al's win, they became the first brothers to take the Brickyard crown.

★ CHAPTER NINE ★

1972–1979

"Any Way You Can Take It"

Al Unser won in 1970 with an average speed of 155.749 miles per hour. A year later, he took the Indy going 157.735 miles per hour, a track record. The record lasted only a year, however, for in 1972, Mark Donohue surpassed it by more than five miles per hour.

As speeds inched toward the 200-mile-per-hour mark, concerns about driver safety grew. Newly designed rear and front wings helped the torpedo-shaped cars hug the track's surface, especially in sharp turns. Still, crashes occurred with frightening regularity; when the track was wet, not even the most seasoned drivers could control their cars in a skid.

Three men lost their lives because of speed and

track conditions in 1973. Driver Art Pollard had just hit 191 miles per hour during qualifiers when his car careened into the wall and flipped. He died an hour later.

Rain delayed the race for a day—and perhaps should have delayed it longer, for the track was slick, leading to a 12-car pileup right after the pace lap. David "Salt" Walther's car was ripped apart, sending fuel and burning wreckage onto nearby spectators. Eleven people in the stands were badly injured, but miraculously, no one in the wreck was killed.

There would be no such miracle for Swede Savage. Rain stopped the race until Wednesday, when the track was deemed safe.

Only it wasn't. In lap 58, Savage lost control, hit the outside wall, ricocheted across the track, and hit the inside wall. His car—what was left of it—burst into flames. Swede died of severe burns. A pit-crew member also died when a fire truck struck him.

The race continued, but when rain fell again late in the day, Gordon Johncock was declared the winner at 133 laps.

New safety standards were put in place after the tragedies of 1973. Fuel tanks were downsized to 40 gallons, which increased the number of pit stops from four to six. This helped safety measures, too, because tires could be changed more often. Speeds were kept in check thanks to a new engine valve.

The field in 1974 included Johnny Rutherford, who had been in 10 previous Indys but had yet to finish. This year, he not only finished, but he beat everyone to the checkered flag. He nearly won the following year, too, but slipped to second place when Bobby Unser passed him during a refueling pit stop.

A sudden heavy downpour ended the race six laps later. Unser wanted to be sure he had the win.

"Is this it?" he radioed from his car.

The pit crew radioed back, "You bet it is!"

Rain worked in Rutherford's favor in 1976. Midway through the 200 laps, the skies opened, making the track a danger zone. Hours later, the contest was finally called off. It was the shortest Indy 500 in history—and for the first time ever, the winner, Rutherford, walked rather than drove to Victory Lane.

"Any way you can take it, I guess," Rutherford joked.

Janet Guthrie, the first woman driver in the Indy 500, had a sense of humor, too. When asked how to succeed in driving, she answered, "Be born rich." Wealth didn't help her in 1977, unfortunately, for she roared around the Speedway just 27 times before a timing-gear failure sidelined her.

Meanwhile, Foyt was driving into the record books. An also-ran since his victory in 1967, he and Johncock were vying for the lead going into the last 20 laps. Then Johncock was knocked out with a broken crankshaft. Foyt sailed through the final miles unchallenged to claim his fourth crown. To celebrate his historic win, he drove a victory lap with Speedway owner Tony Hulman in his car.

That lap turned out to be bittersweet, for Hulman died in late October. But his legacy lives on, for his family still owns and operates the track—and still issues the famous command, "Gentlemen, start your engines."

The 1977 Indy was also the last for longtime hopeful Lloyd Ruby. After 18 consecutive tries, the "greatest driver never to win the Indianapolis 500" retired.

Guthrie made another appearance at the Brickyard in 1978, and this time she not only finished the race but placed ninth. But it was an Unser brother who captured the headlines that day.

Al and Bobby Unser both had two Indy 500 wins. Now Al added a third, beating runner-up Tom Sneva despite a bent wing on his car.

"Unser passed us like we were standing still," Sneva said later.

The Unsers looked unbeatable in the 1979 race—although they almost weren't allowed to compete! Earlier in the year, the United States Auto Club, or USAC, was in a legal battle with a new racing association called the Championship Auto Racing Teams, or CART. The trouble grew when the USAC refused to let six CART drivers enter the Indy 500. Among those six were the Unser brothers and Gordon Johncock. In the end, the courts over-ruled the USAC, and the drivers were allowed to race.

Right from the start, Al and Bobby battled each other for the lead before Al took command. After leading for nearly 100 laps, however, a broken trans-mission ended Al's bid to tie Foyt's four-time Indy win record. Bobby launched a strong campaign, too, but dropped back with gear trouble. That left Sneva, Foyt, and an up-and-coming driver named Rick Mears jockeying for the win.

Late in the race, Mears jumped into the lead. Behind him, Foyt was slowly edging his way through the pack. Mears didn't lose his cool—or his position. When the race ended, it was Mears in first and Foyt a full lap behind in second.

"It's almost like a fairy tale," Mears told reporters later. "This thing happened so quick, it's unbelievable."

Ray Harroun in the single-seater Wasp crosses the finish line to win the first Indianapolis 500, in 1911.

A trio of the best drivers in the 1969 Indianapolis 500—Bobby Unser (car number 1), Mario Andretti (car number 2), and A. J. Foyt Jr. (car number 6)—line up by their cars. Andretti went on to win the race, his only Indy 500 victory.

A. J. Foyt Jr. raises a victory fist as he takes the checkered flag at the 1977 Indianapolis 500.

Car racing is exciting—but also dangerous. Driver Stan Fox is nearly torn from his car after colliding with Eddie Cheever's in the 1995 Indy 500.

The Indianapolis Motor Speedway.

Lee Petty (car number 42) and Johnny Beauchamp (car number 73) race side by side to the finish line in the first Daytona 500, in 1959. Petty wasn't declared the winner until three days later!

In 1981, Richard Petty wins the Daytona 500 for the seventh time, the most victories of any driver in the race's history.

Dale Earnhardt Sr. is nose to tail with his son Dale Earnhardt Jr. during the Daytona 500 on February 18, 2001. It would be the Intimidator's last race.

✶ CHAPTER TEN ✶

1980–1986

Dynasties

Johnny Rutherford had been in 16 Indys since 1963; he'd won two, placed a close second in another, but most often bowed out with car troubles. In 1980, it was his vehicle that gave others trouble.

"The car handles so well I could probably take my hands off the steering wheel down the back-stretch," Rutherford commented before the race.

Thanks to his smooth, lightning-quick ride, Rutherford did just that. As he crossed the finish line in first, he waved at nearby spectators—with both hands!

As good as the car was, Rutherford claimed a lady-bug handed him the win. Rutherford believed lady-bugs brought good luck. So when one landed on him before the race, he figured the Indy was in the bag.

"Those other guys might as well go home," he told his crew.

The 1981 Indianapolis 500 was a battle that really heated up after the race was done. At first, Bobby Unser was declared the victor. But the next day, the USAC announced that Mario Andretti had won! They said that Unser had violated a racing rule when he had passed cars during a yellow flag. As punishment, they handed down a one-lap penalty. That meant Andretti, the runner-up, had crossed the line first.

Unser's team appealed the verdict—and won. Bobby Unser now had three victories and, at age 47, the honor of being the oldest driver ever to win the Indy 500.

The 1982 race began on a somber note with the death of driver Gordon Smiley during the qualifiers. Smiley had been trying to break the 200-mile-per-hour mark when he lost control.

"If you hit wrong, I don't care if you're in a Sherman tank," Foyt said. "It's all over."

It was "all over" for Foyt when a gearshift problem forced him out of contention. Mario Andretti, Roger Mears (Rick's brother), Dale Whittington, and Kevin Cogan were also knocked out after a first-lap crash.

Their loss was Johncock's gain. He sailed across the finish line doing what Smiley had died trying to do—clocking more than 200 miles per hour. Right on his tail was Rick Mears, who came in just sixteen-hundredths of one second behind him. It was one of the closest finishes in recent years.

The following race marked the first father-son competitors in the Indy 500. Al Unser and his son, "Little Al," were running well throughout the first 190 laps. Then Little Al's car ran out of fuel. Al Sr. came close to catching the leader, Tom Sneva, but wound up chasing him over the line 11 seconds later.

In 1984, Al and Little Al were joined by Mario Andretti and his son, Michael. Mario must have been proud of his boy that day, for Michael placed fifth. Mario came in 17th, four places better than Little Al. Al Sr. proved that an old dog still knew some tricks and took third. Rick Mears, meanwhile, earned his second Indy crown with a record-breaking average speed of 163.612.

A record was set in 1985, too, when Danny Sullivan became the first driver to win from the eighth starting position. He nearly didn't finish at all, for in lap 120 his car suddenly spun a full 360 degrees!

"What a dumb mistake!" Sullivan remembered thinking, certain he had just eliminated himself from the race.

But he hadn't! When smoke from his tires cleared, his car was pointed in the right direction. Eighty laps later, he took the checkered flag.

The Indy 500 turned 75 a year after Sullivan's victory. To celebrate, the American Broadcasting Company (ABC) planned to air the entire 500 miles live. Unfortunately, those plans were washed out by heavy rains that postponed the contest for two days. Tom Sneva may have wished to have had yet another delay, for he crashed during the pre-race parade!

After that embarrassing start, the 1986 Indy 500 turned suspenseful. Going into the last 15 laps, three racers were vying for first place. Bobby Rahal screamed past leader Rick Mears. But Kevin Cogan stole his advantage one lap later. A yellow flag forced the three to maintain their positions—but when the green flew, Rahal floored it and sped by Cogan at a mind-numbing 209 miles per hour!

Cogan and Mears tried to match that speed but couldn't. Cogan crossed the line 1.44 seconds after Rahal, with Mears following a scant 0.44 second later. It was the closest one-two-three finish in Brickyard history and, at just under three hours, the shortest duration of any Indy 500 yet.

Records are meant to be broken, however, and the next year, one of the most familiar and popular drivers of Indy history did just that.

★ CHAPTER ELEVEN ★

1987–1992

International Indy

Al Unser Sr. had raced the 500 every year but one since 1965. He'd won back-to-back crowns in 1970 and 1971 and added a third in 1978. He came close to posting a fourth in both 1983 and 1984, only to drop to second and third place those years, respectively. He'd celebrated his brother's three victories and competed against his son in four Indys.

In 1987, he showed them all how to get the job done by running a near-perfect race.

For most of the 200 laps, the 47-year-old bided his time behind the leaders. His patience was finally rewarded in the last hour. First, Mario Andretti was knocked out with car trouble. Then the new leader, Roberto Guerrero, stalled twice in the pits. From then on, it was smooth sailing for Unser—who streaked across the finish line to tie A. J. Foyt Jr. with four Indy wins.

"They called him washed up and retired and all that," Little Al said admiringly. "He's far from that. I've got goose bumps. I'm ecstatic for Dad."

Rick Mears, who once famously said, "To finish first, you must first finish," put his money where his mouth was by finishing—in first—in 1988.

Unser, Foyt, Andretti, Mears, Rutherford, Johncock, Sneva—these were the winning drivers of the Indy 500s of the 1960s, 1970s, and 1980s. They drove for different teams and behind the wheels of different car models. But they all had one thing in common: They were all from the United States.

In 1989, the United States' dominance at the Brickyard ended when Brazilian driver Emerson Fittipaldi charged across the finish line following a second-to-last-lap wheel collision with Little Al. Some thought Fittipaldi had tapped Unser on purpose, as revenge for a crash between the two in another race.

But Little Al disagreed. "What happened was a racing accident, and that's the way it goes," he told the press.

The big news at the Brickyard in 1990 was

record-shattering speeds. In qualifiers, Little Al was a blur of metal at 228 miles per hour, although Fittipaldi took the pole with an overall average speed of 225.3 miles per hour. Unfortunately for the Brazilian, tire troubles kept him from capturing a second consecutive crown.

Fittipaldi's problems were a boon for Arie Luyendyk. A five-time Indy veteran, the Dutchman had never placed higher than sixth. This year, he grabbed international headlines by annihilating the average speed record of 170.722 with a blistering 185.981—a jump of more than 15 miles per hour and fast enough to pulverize the race duration record by 13 minutes! In a race that is often won by seconds, that difference was astonishing.

In 1991, the name Andretti filled up four of the 33 slots of the field. Mario, his son Michael, and his nephew John were joined by Mario's other boy, Jeff. Mario's car was running well until lap 191, when his engine gave out. John finished fifth, and Jeff came in 15th. But it was Michael who nearly added his name to the winner's list.

When Mario's engine trouble brought out the yellow flag, Michael found himself locked in first place alongside Rick Mears. When the green flag waved, they both hit the gas.

Fans were thrilled with their late-lap duel. So was Mears, who had almost missed the race when he crashed 16 days earlier. He had rebounded, however, to claim the pole position. Now he was locked in the closest Indy 500 contest of his career. With his fourth win in sight, he powered his vehicle just slightly ahead of Andretti's—and blazed across the finish line to victory!

"Having a shoot-out at the end and come out on top," Mears said, "that for me is by far more satisfying than having a two-lap lead."

After coming so close, Michael Andretti looked unstoppable in 1992. Then the same bad luck that had dogged his father's Indy 500 career—called the Andretti Curse by some—hit him. Battling high winds, unseasonably cold weather, and a debris-strewn track, as well as other drivers, Michael had the lead going into lap 189 when the unthinkable happened. His car slowed—and then stopped altogether!

A failed fuel pump was to blame, but that didn't matter to Andretti. After leading for 160 of 189 laps, he stood by and watched Little Al claim the win by the smallest margin in Indy history, 0.043 of one second.

The 1992 race was the last run by several popular drivers, including past winners Rick Mears, Gordon Johncock, and Tom Sneva. Also bowing out was A. J. Foyt Jr., who had qualified for an amazing 35 consecutive Indianapolis 500s in his decades-long career.

The 1992 Indy also saw the first woman earn Rookie of the Year. Lyn St. James had been an amateur racer since 1973. In 1992 she became the first female since Janet Guthrie to qualify for the 500. She performed well, finishing in 11th place overall.

The next year, the Brickyard was altered to keep speeds down. All four turns were narrowed, and the inner lane was changed from pavement to grass. That made passing in the turns close to impossible. Rumble strips—grooved pavement that rumbled when driven over—were added to the inside lane to keep drivers from shortcutting over the grass. There was also a completely new pit lane on the inside of the grass lane. Finally, stronger, taller walls and fences were built to surround the outside of the track.

Only time would tell how effective these safety measures were.

⋆ CHAPTER TWELVE ⋆

1993–1999

The Next Generation

The 1993 Indy 500 hosted its first truly international field, with representatives from Japan, Brazil, Sweden, Italy, France, the United Kingdom, Australia, Canada, and Colombia as well as the United States. These drivers handled the Brickyard well: Four of the top five were from countries other than the United States, with previous winner Emerson Fittipaldi claiming his second victory.

A year later, Fittipaldi had a comfortable lead when, with 15 laps remaining, he saw Little Al in front of him. He hit the gas, hoping to lap Unser. But his plan backfired.

"When you run up on the back of another car," Little Al explained, "it sucks all the air away and you lose all your downforce."

Fittipaldi's car wobbled out of control. Moments later—*wham!*—he hit the wall. He was unharmed but out of the race. Little Al avoided the wreckage and motored to his second Indy 500 victory. That win brought the Unser family's total crowns to nine, making Bobby, Al Sr., and Little Al a true driving dynasty.

That same day saw the end of a career for the head of another dynasty. Mario Andretti had been part of the Indy 500 since 1965. Bad luck with cars and crashes had handed him just one victory. After the 1994 race—another that found him bowing out because of mechanical problems—Andretti announced his retirement.

As all professional drivers know, one wrong move can turn a speeding ton of metal into a twisted ton of wreckage. The Speedway had witnessed hundreds of horrific crashes. In the first lap of the 1995 Indy 500, it added another.

Stan Fox's 11th-place starting position was his best in eight trips to the Brickyard. No doubt, he was hoping to make the most of it.

Unfortunately, he may have been too eager. In the first lap, he misjudged turn 1 and ran into the wall. His car exploded on impact. Things went from bad to worse when Eddie Cheever slammed into him. Fox's car flew into the air, crashed down, and disintegrated into thousands of pieces. When the smoke cleared, Fox could be seen in his cockpit, his legs exposed where the front of his car had been ripped away. Miraculously, he was still alive.

There were two other minor crashes that day. After the first, Jacques Villeneuve was given a two-lap penalty for passing the pace car while the yellow flag was still flying. After the second, Scott Goodyear refused to acknowledge the black flag waving him toward the pits. Instead, he continued racing—and earned five penalty laps that dropped him to 14th place. Villeneuve, meanwhile, recovered the lead and won.

The 1996 Indy 500 saw the largest crop of new drivers in the race's history. The reason for the rookie field was the formation of the Indy Racing League, or IRL, by Tony Hulman George, grandson of Tony Hulman and current Speedway owner. The IRL was a direct rival to the CART league. Its close affiliation with George and the Speedway meant that 25 of the 33 starting slots went to IRL teams. First-time Indy 500 drivers filled 17 of those 25 slots.

The one familiar name in the lineup was Unser—not Bobby, Al Sr., or Little Al, but Johnny, son of the late Jerry Unser. Any hope that Johnny would drive to victory that day ended during the parade lap, when his transmission failed.

The winner, Buddy Lazier, undoubtedly benefited from the stripped-down field. Lazier had qualified for three out of seven Indy 500s since 1989. Of those, he never started better than 23rd or finished better than 14th. This time, he started at fifth—and finished in first!

The next year, the Indy 500 had so many starts and stops it was like watching rush hour traffic instead of a race. Rain postponed it for a day. Then an accident before the race stopped the cars before they'd even begun. And with only 15 laps in, the rains returned, and the race was delayed for another day!

Finally, the track was deemed dry, and the cars took off. It was relatively smooth sailing until lap 198, when driver Tony Stewart ran his car up against the wall. Officials halted the race on the assumption that he'd left behind dangerous debris. The drivers prepared to finish the race under the yellow flag.

But when the race resumed, it was the green flag that waved! Most drivers were taken by surprise. Not Arie Luyendyk. He gunned it and roared over the finish line a split second before Scott Goodyear to claim his second title.

To the delight of many Indy fans, the IRL rule that awarded 25 slots to its drivers was gone in 1998. That opened the field to a much wider and more experienced range of racers, leading to a more exciting race overall.

There were still plenty of rookie drivers, however, including the third second-generation of the Unser family. "Getting in this show is all I've ever wanted," Bobby's son Robby told reporters before the race.

With his father, Al Sr., and Little Al watching from the pits and his cousin Johnny racing on the track with him, Robby wove through the pack to take fifth place. Eddie Cheever, the driver who had slammed into Stan Fox three years earlier, survived all 200 laps to take his first and only Indy 500.

The following year found a well-known racing personality entering the winner's circle again. Since his retirement in 1993, team owner A. J. Foyt Jr. had poured his considerable racing knowledge into a new crop of drivers. One of them, Swedish racer Kenny Brack, learned his lessons well. He drove across the finish line ahead of the pack to give Foyt his first Indy crown as an owner.

"You can't ask for anything better than that," Foyt commented with a smile after the race.

★ CHAPTER THIRTEEN ★

2000–2005

The New Century

The first Indianapolis 500s of the new century debuted some of the most exciting drivers in the world. Juan Montoya had been racing since the age of six, when he'd competed in go-karts in his native country of Colombia. In 1999, his rookie year with CART, he won the championship. He drove in his first Indy 500 in 2000—and won that, too, edging out Buddy Lazier by seven seconds.

The winner in 2001 was also a rookie. Like Montoya, Brazilian Helio Castroneves had gotten his start in the go-kart circuit. His lifetime of driving fast and smart showed clearly midway through the race. He picked his way around more experienced Indy 500 racers, including Michael Andretti and

Arie Luyendyk, to take the lead. The race was halted shortly after that because of rain, but when it resumed, Castroneves knew what he had to do.

"I stopped trying to go faster and faster," he recalled later, "because I didn't want to take a chance....I said to myself, 'If you are here [in the lead], it's because you save your car, save your equipment and even yourself so you can go for it.' That's what I did."

The next year, Castroneves went for it again. After nursing a near-empty fuel tank for the last lap, he chugged over the finish line to win a second consecutive Indianapolis 500.

The victory was controversial, however. Paul Tracy, the runner-up, argued that he had passed Castroneves in lap 198 before a yellow caution came out. But officials said that he had passed Castroneves *after* the yellow. Since it's against the rules to pass during a yellow, Tracy was not the winner.

Castroneves, meanwhile, was too busy celebrating to give the matter much attention. The year before, he had shown his joy by climbing a fence near the grandstands. The act earned him the nickname "Spider-Man." Spider-Man repeated his performance in 2002 and was joined by most of his pit crew.

In 2003, the name *Foyt* returned to the lineup. Anthony Joseph Foyt IV, grandson of A. J. Foyt Jr., was celebrating his 19th birthday from behind the wheel in his first 500. He nearly didn't make the grade, however. In his opening qualifier, he spun 180 degrees—and traveled backward at 170 miles per hour before righting the car!

Fortunately, his next run was good enough to earn him a starting slot. In the race, however, inexperience found him finishing in 18th place. Little Al Unser fared better, coming in ninth. Meanwhile, after leading for 28 laps, Michael Andretti fell victim to throttle trouble and ended up with a disappointing 27th-place finish.

The story from Victory Lane that year was inspirational. Up until a few weeks before the race, Brazilian Gil de Ferran had been in the hospital, recovering from severe injuries from a car accident. He not only rebounded in time to drive the Indy, he won it by beating his friend Castroneves.

"In the last few laps, I was thinking, 'Is this really happening?'" de Ferran said.

Bad weather took center stage in 2004 with one of the most ferocious downpours race day had ever seen. Rain delayed the start for two hours, stopped the race in lap 27, and finally ended it for good in lap 180.

The winner, Buddy Rice, was the first American since Eddie Cheever in 1998 to take the crown. "This is unbelievable," he said in an interview afterward.

His win *was* unbelievable. He was in the driver's seat because his team, Rahal-Letterman, needed a replacement for Kenny Brack, who was seriously injured in a crash in late 2003. Rice was in the pole position after qualifying with a speed of 222.024 miles per hour. He took an early lead but lost it after the rain delay. He fell farther behind when he stalled in the pits.

But he didn't give up. Instead, when two accidents eliminated tough competition, he pursued the lead spot relentlessly. When thunderstorms forced track officials to call it quits once and for all, he had chased down the win.

"My God, what a job Buddy did," David Letterman, team owner and television celebrity, exclaimed afterward, "just coming after it, and coming after it, and coming after it."

"This race is supposed to be won by the best car and the best driver," runner-up Tony Kanaan agreed, "and I think it happened."

In 2005, the racing world found a new hero—or heroine, to be exact. Danica Patrick was the fourth woman driver in the Indy 500, following trailblazers Janet Guthrie, Lyn St. James, and, most recently, Sarah Fisher. Patrick electrified fans by posting the best overall speed, a scorching 229.880 miles per hour, in her first practice run. She missed capturing the pole but still earned the fourth position, the best of any woman to date.

And she wasn't done yet. At mile 125, she did what no female driver had ever done—she roared into first place! She fell behind soon after, however, and later was entangled in a four-car crash. Amazingly, she and her car recovered—and she reclaimed the lead! With fewer than 20 laps left to run, fans were wondering if they would witness history that day when Patrick became the first woman to win the Indy 500.

It was not to be, however. Patrick was passed in

lap 194 when she was forced to throttle back to save fuel. She dropped farther behind, but not out. When the race ended, she had taken fourth place behind winner Dan Wheldon. No other woman had ever placed in the top five; only Guthrie, who came in ninth in 1978, had come close.

Patrick returned to the Indy 500 in 2006, but that year her story took a backseat to one of the most incredible finishes the Brickyard had ever witnessed.

★ CHAPTER FOURTEEN ★

2006–2010

The Brickyard's Legends Continue

In 2006, Michael Andretti came out of retirement to race against his son, Marco, who was in the Indy 500 for the first time. Also there were pole sitter Sam Hornish, defending champ Dan Wheldon, and two-time winner Helio Castroneves.

When the green flag waved, Hornish, Wheldon, and Castroneves became locked in a three-way battle for supremacy. Just after the halfway mark, however, Castroneves crashed and was out. Hornish stole Wheldon's lead in lap 130, only to have Wheldon take it back 15 laps later.

Hornish almost left the race when, during a refuel pit stop that recalled Lloyd Ruby's mishap decades earlier, his crew gave him the go-ahead before taking the nozzle out of the tank. Fortunately, the nozzle didn't damage Hornish's car. But he was penalized a lap for not driving through the pit area at the set speed limit!

Meanwhile, the Andrettis were edging ahead. In lap 193, Michael bypassed the pits to claim the top spot. A few laps later, Marco scooted into second place behind him. Hornish sneaked into third.

With three laps remaining, Marco rocketed by his father! Michael didn't challenge his lead. Instead, he tried to block Hornish.

But nothing he did worked. Hornish passed him. Now it was up to Marco to fend off the challenger. And he did, for two and three-quarter laps. Then suddenly—*zoom!*—Hornish gunned his engine coming out of turn 4, flew past Marco, and won!

The elder Andretti couldn't believe his eyes. "Where did Hornish get that speed?" Michael wondered. "It's like he had a button in there to push!"

Hornish took the checkered flag by one of the slimmest margins in Indy history, a mere 0.0635 second ahead of Marco. But as far as Marco was concerned, it could have been six minutes. "They don't remember people who finish second here," he said.

Rain was a major factor again at the 2007 Indianapolis 500, the first to see three women—Danica

Patrick, Sarah Fisher, and rookie Milka Duno—in the lineup. Overnight showers gave way to sunny morning skies that gradually clouded up as race day progressed. By lap 113, a drenching downpour forced officials to fly the red flag.

If the race had been decided then, the top three slots would have gone to Tony Kanaan, Marco Andretti, and Danica Patrick. But it resumed, and one by one, the three leaders dropped behind or out, making way for three new front-runners.

In first was Dario Franchitti. Behind him were Scott Dixon and Helio Castroneves. Castroneves had exchanged the lead with Kanaan several times earlier in the day. Dixon had led three times himself. But any hope he, Castroneves, or anyone else had of surpassing Franchitti died when another fierce thunderstorm ended the race once and for all.

"I'm in shock right now," the newly crowned Franchitti said joyfully. "It was a roller-coaster day."

It was a roller coaster for the three female drivers, too. After hanging at the front of the pack for much of the shortened race, Patrick ended in eighth place. Fisher finished in 21st. Duno, unfortunately, crashed in lap 65 and wound up in 31st.

All three returned for another try in 2008, but

none of them succeeded in capturing the elusive crown. Patrick had a stormy moment, however, when Ryan Briscoe clipped her car while leaving the pits. She was unharmed but furious at what she thought was an avoidable accident. She stalked toward Briscoe's pit to confront him. Security intervened before there was an incident.

Meanwhile, Tony Kanaan set a 500 record by taking the lead for the seventh consecutive year. But his dream of winning was dashed when he was squeezed high into turn 4. He barreled into Fisher, who was a lap behind. Both cars were totaled.

The end of the race belonged to Scott Dixon, who fought off onslaughts by Vitor Meira, Marco Andretti, and Helio Castroneves throughout the final 24 laps. His victory marked the 19th time the pole sitter had won the Indy—and the first time a driver from New Zealand had taken the checkered flag.

Dixon was back for the 2009 Indy 500, as were favorites Castroneves, Andretti, Meira, Patrick, Franchitti, and Kanaan. Unfortunately for Andretti fans, Marco was bumped from contention in a crash seconds after the race began.

Crashes took out other racers, too. Tony Kanaan

was in third when his steering system gave out. He lost control, careened off the wall, and slammed into a barrier with unbelievable force.

"I knew it was going to be a big one," Kanaan said shakily. "I'm pretty beat up."

Vitor Meira and Rafael Matos were worse than "beat up" when their wheels touched late in the race. Meira spun out in front of Matos, who pushed Meira up against the outside wall. Meira flipped up onto two wheels and rode the wall backward for several yards before landing hard. Both drivers were badly injured.

The race resumed after the wreckage was cleared. Castroneves was out in front. Wheldon and Patrick gave chase but couldn't catch the wily Brazilian. Castroneves zoomed over the finish line to join the ranks of three-time Indy 500 winners. Wheldon claimed second, and Danica Patrick became the first woman to make the top three.

"I feel honored to be in this category of drivers," Castroneves declared to the press after his customary Spider-Man climb. "I think my tears speak for everything!"

Dario Franchitti felt equally honored a year later. That's when he drove into Victory Lane for the second time in his career. His win came under the yellow caution flag that was flying because of a spectacular last-lap crash by Mike Conway. If not for that flag, Franchitti might not have won—his fuel was down to less than two gallons when he zoomed over the finish line!

Fiery crashes, photo finishes, driving duels, and daring drivers: It's the stuff that's made the Indy 500 one of the most legendary races of all time. But it's not the only long-distance race to capture the hearts of fans. Far south of Indianapolis is another speedway—and another 500.

THE DAYTONA 500

☆ CHAPTER FIFTEEN ☆

1902–1959

From the Flats of Daytona Beach

The Indianapolis Motor Speedway is set in the heart of Indiana. When it was built, it was surrounded by acres of flat farmland.

The Daytona International Speedway, on the other hand, was constructed near a beach on the eastern coast of Florida. In fact, before there was a Speedway, car races were held on the sand flats between Daytona Beach and nearby Ormond Beach.

Back in the late 1800s and early 1900s, Daytona Beach was a popular vacation spot for wealthy businessmen and their families. These men challenged one another to sailboat races and, after the automobile was invented, car races. The first recorded automobile races at Daytona Beach were speed trials held in 1902. The winner was car manufacturer

Ransom E. Olds, whose Oldsmobile was clocked at 57 miles per hour.

In the years that followed, Daytona Beach continued to attract people who could afford the luxurious "horseless carriages." The course changed from all sand to sand and pavement, thanks to a segment of nearby highway. By the mid-1910s, anyone who wanted to experience the thrill of car racing knew that Daytona Beach was the place to go.

World War I temporarily interrupted the events at Daytona Beach, just as it had stopped the races in Indianapolis and elsewhere in the world. When the war ended in 1918, however, interest in cars and racing skyrocketed as never before.

The next decades saw several land-speed records set and shattered at Daytona Beach. Ralph DePalma hit 149.875 miles per hour in 1919. Tommy Milton clocked 156.030 a year later. Seven years after that, Henry Segrave broke the 200 mark with a speed of 203.792. But the true king of speed at Daytona Beach was Malcolm Campbell. He bested his own records three years in a row, starting with 246.090 miles per hour in 1931 and ending at 276.820 in 1934.

By then, the speed trials at Daytona Beach were

so popular that the area could no longer accommodate the crowds or the racers. The events were moved to Utah in 1935, where the Bonneville Salt Flats offered more room and more consistently stable surfaces on which to race.

But the Daytona Beach course wasn't abandoned altogether. Instead, the city held stock car races on the flats. The first two, held in 1936 and 1937, were financial bombs. That's when Florida businessman and sometime–stock car racer William "Big Bill" France stepped in.

Big Bill promoted and organized the Daytona Beach races for the next four years. The events grew more popular with each running. In 1942, however, all came to a stop when the United States entered World War II following the bombing of Pearl Harbor.

When the war ended in 1945, Bill France picked up where he left off—or tried to, anyway. By 1947, however, he realized that if racing was to truly succeed at Daytona Beach, he would need help. On December 12, France headed up a meeting with stock car drivers, mechanics, race car owners, and other interested parties to discuss the future of car racing.

During the meeting, France outlined his main

idea for that future. He knew that open-wheeled racing had a huge following. But he believed there was another segment of the population that would prefer to see something more familiar on the track.

"Plain, ordinary working people have to be able to associate with the cars," France declared. "Standard street stock cars are what we should be running."

The other men present agreed. With Bill France at the helm, they founded a new governing body, the National Association for Stock Car Auto Racing, or NASCAR, on February 21, 1948. NASCAR set down rules aimed at keeping competition even and financial compensation fair. The group established a points system, too, as a way of rating drivers over a year of events.

NASCAR sanctioned 52 races in 1948, but because brand-new stock cars weren't readily available then, these races featured Modifieds—that is, stock cars altered to give them a competitive edge. The winner of the first NASCAR Modified race was Red Byron, who later went on to capture the Modified championship.

NASCAR's first "strictly stock" car race took

place at the Charlotte Speedway in North Carolina on June 19, 1949. Jim Roper, a driver from Kansas who got his start in midget cars, won by default after the first man across the finish line, Glenn Dunnaway, was found to have altered his car.

Several other Strictly Stock NASCAR events followed, each more popular than the one before it. In recognition of the sport's growing appeal, France changed the series name from Strictly Stock to the Grand National Series.

On Labor Day in 1950, the Grand National held its biggest race yet—a 500-miler at the Darlington Raceway in South Carolina. Seventy-five drivers lined up on the mile-and-a-quarter-long paved track. Six hours later, Johnny Mantz crossed the finish line to win with an average speed of 76 miles per hour.

NASCAR continued to expand throughout the 1950s. That expansion included a brand-new venue in NASCAR's birthplace. Bill France had long wanted Daytona Beach to have its own race course. On February 22, 1959, that dream became a reality. The Daytona International Speedway, a two-and-a-half-mile paved oval, opened its gates for the inaugural Daytona 500.

"There have been other tracks that have separated the men from the boys," one driver said when he saw the Speedway. "This is the track that will separate the brave from the weak after the boys have gone."

★ CHAPTER SIXTEEN ★

1959–1961

The First 500 and the First Petty

The Indianapolis 500 has its dynasties—the Foyts, the Unsers, the Andrettis, and others. NASCAR's Daytona 500 has its "first families," too. One of the best known is the Pettys.

Lee Petty was the first in the family to drive for NASCAR. Born in 1914 in North Carolina, he didn't grow up racing but discovered his love of the sport when he was 35. That's when he took part in NASCAR's first race at the Charlotte Speedway. He didn't do very well, however. In fact, he rolled his family's Buick, totaling it!

"I was just sitting there thinking about having to go back home and explain to my wife where I'd been with the car," he later joked.

Some drivers might have walked away then, but

not Petty. He bought a new, lighter-weight car and entered two more races in 1949. He came in seventh out of 45 cars in the first race and second in the other.

Petty continued to compete and improve. In 1954, he entered 34 races, captured the pole position in three, and won two of those three to become the Grand National champion. Four years and two more championships later, he was looking ahead to the most highly anticipated race NASCAR had ever sponsored: the Daytona 500.

Petty had driven on Big Bill France's superspeedway two days earlier in the Daytona 500 qualifier. That race was 40 laps long, a fraction of the distance of the upcoming 500. Petty had started in 14th place and finished in eighth.

He was hoping to do better on race day.

The inaugural Daytona 500 took place on February 22, 1959, before a boisterous crowd of more than 40,000 fans. The green flag flew at noon. Pole winner Bob Welborn jumped in front right away but was soon challenged by "Tiger" Tom Pistone and Joe Weatherly.

All three fell behind in lap 23, however, when fan favorite Edward Glenn "Fireball" Roberts burned rubber past them. Roberts held the lead for the next 20 circuits. He might have stayed there had a broken fuel pump not sent him out for good in lap 57.

That gave Johnny Beauchamp the chance he'd been looking for. He zoomed ahead to claim the lead, only to lose it to Pistone, who himself struggled to stay in front when Jack Smith roared up from behind. Smith eventually stole Pistone's position, but Pistone didn't give up so easily. He and Smith traded the lead for the next 50 laps.

Meanwhile, Lee Petty, in car number 42, was watching and waiting. So was Beauchamp. In lap 107, Beauchamp made his move—right into the front! Smith gave chase and regained the lead nine laps later. Beauchamp needed 31 turns around the course to catch Smith, but he finally succeeded.

He held the first-place spot only for one lap, however, before Lee Petty took charge of the field. From then on, the inaugural Daytona 500 was an edge-of-the-seat battle between Petty and Beauchamp. They traded the lead a total of 11 times between laps 150 and 197. Petty had the advantage then, but Beauchamp fought back and drew alongside car number 42. At the end of the final three laps, Beauchamp crossed the finish line first!

At least, that's what the officials ruled when the checkered flag waved. But Petty didn't buy it.

"I had Beauchamp by a good two feet," Petty stated. "I know I won."

Fireball Roberts had witnessed the race's end right beside the finish line. He agreed with Petty. "There was no doubt about it," he said. "Petty won."

Still, officials weren't sure. Bill France gathered all the photographic evidence he could find and reviewed it with the officials. It took them three days to come to a conclusion. Only then did they make their announcement: Lee Petty was the winner!

Petty participated in the Daytona 500 again in 1960 and came in fourth after leading for 14 laps. In 1961, his chance for a third run at the crown was cut short by a devastating accident during the race's qualifiers.

Also in the accident was Johnny Beauchamp. As the two drivers entered a turn, they locked bumpers. Out of control, they barreled up the banking, through the fence, and out of the track. Video of the wreck shows Petty's car sailing through the air upside down before landing in a smoking tangle with Beauchamp's car.

Amazingly, both drivers survived—a fact that

was nothing short of miraculous for one witness in particular.

Richard Petty, Lee's son, was also a NASCAR driver. The 1959 Rookie of the Year, he had been in the first Daytona 500 but had been sidelined with engine problems after just eight laps. Still, he had the thrill of watching the last-lap duel between his father and Beauchamp and delighted in the elder Petty's victory.

Now, he faced a nightmarish scene. "There wasn't anything left of either car," he wrote in his autobiography. "There was blood everywhere, and they had just taken Daddy out of the car and were putting him in the back of an ambulance. He was lifeless."

It took many months, but Lee Petty finally recovered from his injuries. He got behind the wheel of his race car again, too, although, according to his son, "it sure wasn't the Lee Petty of old."

Three years later, the three-time Grand National champion and winner of the inaugural Daytona 500 retired from racing. He stayed in the game, however, as the owner of Petty Enterprises, the team that went on to manage one of the most successful drivers in NASCAR's history: Richard Petty.

★ CHAPTER SEVENTEEN ★

1962–1971

King Richard

Richard Lee Petty started in his first NASCAR race on July 18, 1958. He didn't finish, because he was sent into the fences after being bumped by another car. The driver of that other car? Lee Petty!

Richard drove in eight more events that year. The next year, he entered 21 races and took nine top-10 finishes, six of which were top five. He finished as Rookie of the Year.

Petty improved with each passing season. In 1963, he grabbed eight poles and won a whopping 14 out of 54 races. Then in 1964, he did what his famous father had done—win the Daytona 500.

The field that day was loaded with talent. Ned Jarrett, Robert Glenn "Junior" Johnson, Fireball Roberts, and Ralph Earnhardt were NASCAR veterans. Johnny Rutherford, A. J. Foyt Jr., and Parnelli Jones had temporarily traded in their open-wheeled single-seaters for stock cars. Up-and-comers Cale Yarborough and David Pearson were eager to test their skills against the greats, on the greatest course in the NASCAR circuit.

Richard Petty beat them all. Starting from the second slot, he roared past pole sitter Paul Goldsmith and into the lead in lap 2. Others took command in the first quarter of the race, including Foyt, who led for a single lap. But in lap 52, Petty made his way to the front of the pack again—and that's where he stayed for the remainder of the race!

When the checkered flag flew over car number 43, Petty had led for 184 of the 200 laps. Runner-up Jimmy Pardue took an entire lap plus nine seconds to cross the line after him.

The Daytona 500 was Petty's second victory out of seven races so far in the season. In the months ahead, he won seven more times. To no one's surprise, he was the Grand National champion that year, making it four times in 10 years that a driver with the last name Petty earned the NASCAR title.

But while 1964 was a year of triumph for Richard and Petty Enterprises, it was one of tragedy for other well-known drivers. Fireball Roberts, who had always hated his nickname because he feared fire, died in a fiery crash in May. Dave MacDonald and Eddie Sachs also perished in May when their cars collided during the Indy 500. Within the next year, three others were killed in separate incidents while testing tires.

These deaths were a wake-up call for NASCAR. The association soon mandated new safety measures such as fire-retardant suits and crash helmets.

Richard Petty took part in 61 NASCAR races in 1964. In 1965, he drove in just 14. His scaled-back schedule was the result of a boycott against NASCAR.

Petty had won the Daytona 500 with a Hemi, Chrysler's new and very powerful engine, in his car. He thought the engine should be welcomed as an exciting improvement to stock car racing. NASCAR disagreed. In protest, Petty switched to drag racing until NASCAR finally lifted the Hemi ban in late July. He then proceeded to tear up the field, winning the pole in half of his 14 races and taking the checkered flag in four.

Petty won a second Daytona 500 in 1966, but the next season was his best ever. Forty-eight races, 27 wins, 38 top fives, 40 top 10s, and 18 poles—his stats were absolutely staggering! The one disappointment had to have been at the Daytona 500 when, after 193 laps, his engine quit.

That same race saw a familiar yet unexpected name in the lineup. Mario Andretti was known for racing Indy cars. But in 1967, he decided to see what he could do behind the wheel of a stock car.

What he did was crush the competition for 112 out of 200 laps! "You don't baby a car at Daytona like you do at Indy," he said from the Speedway's Victory Lane. "It's flat out."

"Flat out" is how Cale Yarborough and LeeRoy Yarbrough drove the next Daytona 500. The two were neck and neck going into the last laps when Cale swept around LeeRoy. He stayed just far enough ahead to capture the win by a 1.3-second margin. LeeRoy had his own photo-finish victory the next year, however, besting Charlie Glotzbach. Phenom Pete Hamilton came out of nowhere to claim the crown in 1970, charging past Glotzbach and future winner David Pearson before the largest crowd the Speedway had ever seen.

Big changes were in store for NASCAR in the months after Hamilton's win. Car companies such as Ford, Chrysler, and Pontiac had long sponsored teams but now wanted more control over the sport itself. When Bill France refused to let them have a bigger voice, they started to withdraw their funding. That left NASCAR in financial difficulty.

Then help stepped in. R. J. Reynolds Tobacco Company, maker of cigarettes, had long been interested in stock car racing. Now the company and NASCAR came to an arrangement that suited them both. Reynolds provided sponsorship and money; NASCAR changed the name of its stock car circuit from the Grand National Championship to the Winston Cup Series, after Reynolds's Winston cigarette brand.

On Valentine's Day 1971, Richard Petty ran a sweetheart of a race at the Daytona International Speedway. The finish looked to be a three-way battle among Petty, Donnie Allison, and David Pearson—until lap 182. That's when Petty roared into the lead once and for all. With an average speed of 144.462 miles per hour and seven cautions, it took him nearly three and a half hours to complete the race. When he did, he made history as the first driver to win three Daytona 500s.

And his history was just beginning.

★ CHAPTER EIGHTEEN ★

1972–1979

Dramatic Duels and Flying Fists

Richard Petty had set an average speed record of 160.927 at the 1966 Daytona 500. In 1972, versatile racer A. J. Foyt Jr., winner of three Indy 500s and Formula 1's 24 Hours of Le Mans, won the number-one stock car race with a speed of 161.550 miles per hour.

What did Petty think of Foyt? "He fit right in," the lanky Texan said.

Petty himself didn't finish the 1972 race, because a faulty valve sidelined him midway through. But he cleaned up the next two years, becoming the first NASCAR driver to win back-to-back Daytona 500s.

Donnie Allison was his biggest challenger in the second of those victories. The two traded the lead an unbelievable 16 times in the second half of the race. Allison nearly drove off with the win when one of Petty's tires blew. But Petty made it to the pits and after a quick change roared back into contention. His first-place position was assured when Allison's own tire shredded!

Ten laps later, Petty took the checkered flag. When asked what he had left to do now that he had five Daytona victories, Petty drawled, "Go after number six."

That 1974 race was shorter than usual because the nation was in the midst of an energy crisis. Some people complained that car racing was a waste of fuel. So Bill France cut 50 miles off the Daytona 500—although he didn't change the name to the Daytona 450.

The 500 was back to 500 miles the following year. Petty, David Pearson, Bobby and Donnie Allison, Cale Yarborough, and A. J. Foyt Jr. were all looking to add another title or post their first win. But the victory landed in the lap of Benny Parsons when Pearson's car spun out with just two laps remaining!

Pearson, Petty, and Parsons were locked in a last-lap, three-way battle at the 1976 Daytona 500. Petty had two car lengths on Pearson, with Parsons trailing. Then Pearson drove tight onto Petty's back bumper and swooped down to the inside to edge the leader out.

Still, Petty wasn't about to let Pearson win without a fight. As they entered the final turn, he crowded Pearson to the outside wall. But he misjudged the distance between their cars.

Wham!

With the finish line just a hundred yards ahead, Pearson spun nose first into the outside wall. Petty skidded sideways down the track and hit the same wall farther down. Pearson rebounded across the lanes into the infield grass, all the while screaming, "Where's Petty? Where's Petty?" into his radio.

Petty was heading to the infield, going backward! "He's going to win the race!" announcer Jim McKay yelled. "He's going to win it spinning!"

Then, seconds later—"No! He did not make it!"

With just 50 feet to go, Petty was stalled in the grass!

"Go, go, go!" Pearson's pit boss cried.

Pearson chugged by as Petty's crew raced toward him and began to push. With the fans and announcers going crazy, Pearson hit the pavement and crossed the finish line!

Petty crossed it, too, taking second just before

Benny Parsons finished. His dream of winning Daytona 500 number six would have to wait another year.

That year finally came in 1979. Cale Yarborough had taken his second Daytona win in 1977. The following February was a Cinderella story for Bobby Allison, who entered with a 67-race losing streak. During the qualifiers, he wrecked. But when the 500 ended, he'd roared ahead of his competitors to win his first Daytona.

Track conditions for the next year's race were slick thanks to a night of rain. But the race went ahead as scheduled because, for the first time ever, it was being telecast live from start to finish.

And what a finish! Going into the final lap, Donnie Allison looked good to add his name to the winner's list. But behind him was Cale Yarborough. He began drafting behind Allison and, in the backstretch toward the finish, tried to whip around him.

Allison refused to let him pass. Instead, he maneuvered Yarborough toward the muddy infield grass. Then disaster struck. Yarborough's left tires slipped. He collided with Allison. Allison slid and bumped back. Yarborough knocked into him again. Then the cars locked up and, out of control, streaked across the lanes, up the turn slope, and into the outside wall!

That opened the way for Richard Petty, in third, and Darrell Waltrip, in fourth. The two dueled for the lead in the final lap. Petty edged him out with a spectacular dash to the finish line to win his sixth Daytona!

Few people were watching the race's end, however. Instead, all eyes and cameras were trained on the drama in the infield.

After hitting the wall, Yarborough and Donnie Allison had spun back into the grass. Both were out of their cars, arguing loudly. Suddenly, Bobby Allison roared up. Moments later, a brawl broke out between the Allison brothers and Yarborough!

"I jumped out of the car," Bobby said later, "... knowing I had to address it right then or run from Cale the rest of my life. And with that, Cale went to beating on my fist with his nose."

The fistfight was captured on national television. The *New York Times* ran the story on the front page of its sports section. People who had never been interested in NASCAR were suddenly buzzing about the infield melee.

Yarborough was disgusted with the whole

incident, although he later acknowledged the fight boosted NASCAR's popularity. "People looked at that and said, 'These boys are real people, and they do real things,'" he said. "I think it's one of the biggest things that ever happened in the sport. It got people's attention."

★ CHAPTER NINETEEN ★

1980–1989

"I've Won the Daytona!"

In Daytona 500s past, Buddy Baker had been a "close-but-no-cigar" driver. In 1980, while on his way to shattering A. J. Foyt Jr.'s long-standing speed record with a blistering 177.602 miles per hour average, he finally saw the checkered flag fly over his car.

Richard Petty set a possibly unattainable record the following year when he drove into Victory Lane a seventh time. Amazingly, Petty hadn't had the lead all day when, in the 175th lap, front-runner Bobby Allison ran out of fuel before reaching his pits. Despite dangerously worn tires, Petty only refueled during his own pit stop. Moments later, he grabbed the lead and didn't look back.

"It was a follow-the-leader deal," the Texan quipped, "and the deal was we didn't follow."

Bobby Allison and Cale Yarborough duked it out

again in 1982—but with their cars, not their fists. Allison won the battle by 22.87 seconds.

Yarborough flexed his muscle in the 1983 qualifiers, where he posted the fastest-ever lap on the track with a speed of 200.503 miles per hour. One lap later, however, he flipped his speedster, totaling it!

"I don't believe I've ever felt as low," he recalled.

Luckily, Yarborough had a good backup car. In the last lap, it powered him from second to first with slingshot move past Buddy Baker, giving him his third Daytona victory. A year later, fans might have thought they were experiencing déjà vu when they saw him work the same maneuver in the same lap with the same conclusion—except this time, he used his power play to beat Dale Earnhardt, not Buddy Baker.

Earnhardt was a familiar face in the Winston Cup Series. He had first gained notice as Rookie of the Year in 1979. In 1980, he was crowned Winston Cup champion, the only driver to ever win both titles back-to-back. He continued to rake in victories in the years that followed—except at the Daytona 500. Car trouble or better racers edged him out each year, including 1985.

That year's Daytona belonged to "Awesome Bill from Dawsonville." True to his nickname, Bill

Elliott drove an awesome race, outdriving and out-lasting a lineup that included past winners Richard Petty, Benny Parsons, A. J. Foyt Jr., Bobby Allison, and Cale Yarborough. His rocket-fast pace was the reason for his success.

"He played 'catch me if you can,'" said Allison, "and nobody could."

Nobody could catch Geoff Bodine the next year, either, although Dale Earnhardt came very close. Eight miles from the finish, Earnhardt was bumper to bumper with Bodine when he had to refuel. Something went wrong during the stop, however, because when Earnhardt stepped on the gas, his engine blew up!

"If we'd had even a gallon or two left, we'd have made it," Earnhardt said woefully.

Bodine learned what it felt like to run out of fuel when his tank dried up with just three laps remaining the next year. With Bodine out of the way, Elliott took the checkered flag. Unlike his first victory, which was won on speed, this race came courtesy of skillful driving and lightning-quick pit stops.

"That's what won it for us," Elliott said, praising the crew who got him in and out of the pits in 6.3 seconds in his final stop.

In 1988, experience beat out youth in a classic father-son duel. Bobby Allison's son Davey had failed to qualify for either the 1985 or 1986 Daytona 500. In 1987, he finished in 27th place, 21 slots behind his father. Now he finished behind his father again, but in second to Bobby's first-place spot!

"Since I was a kid, I've dreamed of battling to the wire, finishing one-two with my dad," Davey said. "The only difference was, I wanted him to finish second."

While the Allison family was driving into Victory Lane, Richard Petty was being treated for injuries at the hospital.

Midway through the race, Petty's car skidded and became airborne while coming out of a turn. It landed and flipped against the outside fence several times. The fence ripped it to shreds, sending debris flying in all directions. Then the car dropped to the ground only to roll, barrel style, before being smashed into by Brett Bodine and A. J. Foyt Jr. When the vehicle finally stopped moving, more parts were on the ground than on the frame.

Petty blacked out but miraculously suffered only a broken leg.

The final Daytona 500 of the 1980s was a nail-biter for Darrell Waltrip. He'd driven in the race 17 times and come close five times only to see his car fail in the final miles. This year, he dodged two race-ending bullets. The first came midway through the event when 10 cars piled up in a tremendous crash right in front of him! Somehow, he managed to steer clear and keep going.

Later, with just two laps to go, he was on the brink of success when his fuel-pressure gauge suddenly plummeted to zero!

But was he really out of gas? His pit crew chief didn't think so. He urged Waltrip to give the car a little shake and see what happened. Waltrip drafted behind every car he could. Going into the final lap, he squeezed every drop of fuel out of the tank—and sputtered across the line in first place!

"I've won the Daytona 500! I've won the Daytona 500!" he screamed joyfully as he leaped out of his car and did a little dance (later known as the "Icky Shuffle" because it was so awful). "This *is* Daytona, isn't it? Don't lie to me! I'm not dreaming, am I?"

He wasn't dreaming—after nearly two decades of trying, Waltrip had won the 31st Daytona 500 on a thimbleful of gas.

★ CHAPTER TWENTY ★

1990–2001

Hello, Good-bye

They called him "the Intimidator." If he fixed a steely glare at you from behind his signature sunglasses, you might shrink back a little—at least until his huge grin showed up beneath his handlebar mustache.

Dale Earnhardt got his nickname for his aggressive driving style. The son of NASCAR driver Ralph Earnhardt, Dale grew up with stock car racing. Rookie of the Year and seven-time Winston Cup champ, he was one of best drivers ever.

Yet after 12 years of racing, he hadn't won the Great American Race. He'd come close, though.

The 1990 Daytona 500 welcomed NASCAR's finest to the lineup. Also, there were lesser-known drivers like Derrike Cope, who had yet to win a single event in his seven years of NASCAR.

When the green flag waved, the Intimidator took over almost immediately. While he gave up the lead several times, he commanded the course for 155 of 199 laps. Victory seemed certain.

Then, on the last turn of lap 200, the unthinkable happened. Earnhardt ran over a piece of debris! "I heard it hit the bottom of the car, and then it hit the tire and the tire went," he said.

Earnhardt went, too—swerving into the wall right in front of the grandstands. He righted himself, but not in time to take what should have been his first Daytona 500 title. That honor went to Cope, who had sneaked into second at the very end of the race.

"You can't kick the car and cry and pout and lay down and squall and bawl," Earnhardt said matter-of-factly. "We just ran short of luck today."

Earnhardt ran short of luck other days at Daytona, too. In 1991, he spun out with two laps to go. He was wiped out in a 14-car pileup in 1992. The next year, the first name *Dale* was finally etched onto the trophy cup. The last name, however, was *Jarrett*, not *Earnhardt*.

Jarrett's father, Ned, was in the announcer's booth that day. When his son took the lead in the final lap, he began to urge him on.

"Come on, Dale! Go, baby, go!" Then, as if his microphone was connected to Dale's radio headset, he let out a stream of advice on how to stay in front. And finally—"He's gonna make it! Dale Jarrett is going to win the Daytona 500!"

That February race was the Daytona debut of rookie Jeff Gordon. The 21-year-old had been in just one other NASCAR event in late 1992, where he crashed after 164 laps. Now he qualified for the third starting position, led for two laps, and finished in fifth place behind veterans Jarrett, Earnhardt, Bodine, and Hut Stricklin—not bad for his second career race! Not bad became one better for Gordon the following year, when he crossed the finish line in fourth place.

That Daytona went to Sterling Marlin. In 17 years, Marlin had never won a race. His father, Coo Coo Marlin, had retired without a single victory in his 14-year career. Had there been even one more lap to go in the 1994 race, Sterling might not have won this one, either. His car ran out of fuel on his way to Victory Lane and had to be pushed the final yards!

Marlin had the magic touch again the next year, too, becoming only the third driver to win back-to-back Daytona 500s. Gordon had been a contender that race, but a problem in the pits slowed him down. Earnhardt took charge for 23 of the last laps but couldn't fend off Marlin when it counted the most.

"Sterling deserved to win," Earnhardt acknowledged, adding, "I'm not supposed to win the [darn] thing, I don't reckon."

He had reckoned right—for the next two years, anyway. The 1996 race was a replay of the 1992 one, with two Dales coming in one-two—first Jarrett, then Earnhardt. In 1997, Jeff Gordon made good on a promise to his team leader, Rick Hendrick, who was battling leukemia. The night before the event, Gordon told Hendrick he was going to win. And that's just what he did, although the way he did it left the Intimidator steaming mad.

Gordon and Earnhardt were vying for the lead in lap 189. Going into turn 2, Gordon inched Earnhardt toward the outside wall and then dropped to the inside. Earnhardt's car touched the concrete, skidded back, and bumped into Gordon's car. Meanwhile, Jarrett had come up fast on Earnhardt's bumper and tapped him. As the Intimidator rolled out of control, he was hit by Ernie Irvan and spun wildly into the grassy infield!

Remarkably, Earnhardt emerged unscathed. In fact, he finished the race! Gordon may have become the youngest driver ever to win the 500, but Earnhardt won everyone's hearts with his gutsy determination.

"He's invincible," marveled fellow driver Darrell Waltrip.

In 1998, Earnhardt wasn't just invincible—he was a victor. "We won it! We won it! We won it!" he bellowed as he jumped from car number 3, a mile-wide grin on his face.

It would be Earnhardt's only victory at the Daytona 500. In 1999, he came in 0.128 second behind Jeff Gordon. The next year's race was a contest of wills between two Dale Earnhardts. Dale Jr. was driving in his first Daytona 500 while his father was trying for a second win. But it was a third Dale—Dale Jarrett—who won.

Earnhardt Sr. made a prediction before the 2001 Daytona 500. "I think it's gonna be some exciting racing," he told news reporters. "Gonna see something you'd probably never seen."

His prediction came true in the worst possible way.

When the race began, familiar names like Elliott,

Marlin, and Earnhardt (Sr. and Jr.) traded the front spot with less-familiar drivers such as Ward Burton and Mike Skinner. Jeff Gordon joined the pack leaders midway through, as did Michael Waltrip, younger brother of Darrell. With so many lead changes, it was anybody's guess who would emerge victorious.

Midway through the final lap, the Intimidator was in fourth place. Then, at turn 3, something went very, very wrong.

Sterling Marlin nudged Earnhardt Sr.'s back panel. Earnhardt's nose turned up the embankment of turn 4. Moments later, he crashed headfirst into the outside wall. Driver Ken Schrader slammed into him. Locked together, they drifted slowly down the slope to the infield.

Shaken but not seriously hurt, Schrader got out of his car.

Earnhardt did not. He was cut free from his car and rushed to the hospital.

Hours later, NASCAR president Mike Helton appeared on television. "Undoubtedly this is one of the toughest announcements I've personally had to make," he said grimly. "We've lost Dale Earnhardt."

★ CHAPTER TWENTY-ONE ★

2002–2010

Victory Lane and Beyond

In 2002, Sterling Marlin was battling Jeff Gordon for first when their bumpers met. Gordon spun out, while behind him cars plowed into one another across the track. The red flag came out, halting the race so the course could be cleared.

During the stop, Marlin got out of his car to straighten a bent fender. Track officials ordered him back in. Then they ordered him to the rear of the pack for making an illegal pit stop! Instead of taking his third crown, Marlin watched Ward Burton cruise into Victory Lane.

The 2003 Daytona was stopped in lap 109 on account of rain. An hour later, while sitting with his wife in his car on pit row, Michael Waltrip, winner of the 2001 Daytona 500, was awarded his second crown.

"We were just enjoying a day in the rain in Florida," Waltrip joked.

The next year saw some big changes in NASCAR. Gone was the name Winston Cup, replaced by the series' new sponsor, Sprint-Nextel. There was a new format to determine the series' champion, too: "The Chase for the Championship."

NASCAR awards points to drivers for every race: the better the driver's finish, the higher the point value. Before the 2004 season, the driver with the most points overall was named the champion.

The new Chase format made the bid for champion status more exciting by narrowing the field after 26 races to the 12 top point earners. Whichever of the 12 emerged with the greatest point total after the last 10 races was named the Sprint Cup champ.

The first race in the 2004 Chase was the Daytona 500. For some fans, it was the dullest in Speedway history, with little bumper-to-bumper competition and only one major crash.

But for the Earnhardt family, it was one of the best, for Dale Jr. took the checkered flag six years to the day after his father's win.

"Considering what this kid went through losing his father here," said runner-up Tony Stewart, "it's nice to see him get his victory here, too."

Cautions hampered the 2005 Daytona 500. Most of the incidents were minor, but late in the race there were back-to-back Big Ones—a term used in NASCAR to describe a crash involving eight or more cars. Eleven drivers were knocked out in the first; eight left the field after the second.

When the yellow flag flew through lap 200, the race was completed under NASCAR's new green-white-checkered-flag rule. According to the rule, a race running under a caution at the last lap is extended under the green flag for two extra laps. The white flag is flown to indicate one lap remaining; the checkered flag waves over the winner. The new rule made finishes more exciting because drivers could go full speed and pass.

Jeff Gordon took his third Daytona victory after that green-white-checkered flag. The next year, he nearly knocked himself and Tony Stewart out of contention when he edged Stewart up the slope and into the wall at turn 2. Stewart himself caused a crash later when he crowded another driver into the grassy infield. For that maneuver, he was sent to the back courtesy of a new NASCAR penalty against overly aggressive—and potentially dangerous—driving. Interestingly, Stewart had first suggested the penalty after suffering from such action a week earlier!

The 2006 race belonged to Jimmie Johnson, an outstanding driver who had won 18 races in just four years. "Jeff Gordon...Tony Stewart, Dale Jr., that's great company," Johnson said. "I'm honored to be up here as a champion of the Daytona 500 with these guys."

The "guys" added a new name to the list in 2007. Kevin Harvick had won seven national and two Grand National go-kart championships before being given the late Dale Earnhardt's place on Earnhardt's team. By 2006, he had demolished much of the Sprint Cup competition, winning or placing in the top 10 in 76 of the 214 events.

The 2007 Daytona 500 was his fifth attempt to win the Great American Race. He'd finished in fourth twice. This time, he was looking to conquer the course.

Several yellow flags slowed the field but eliminated few. Then came the Big One: an eight-car smashup with just 13 laps left to go. When the wreckage cleared, the surviving drivers went all out, only to be slowed yet again in lap 197 when five more cars crashed! This accident led to a thrilling green-white-checkered finish.

The remaining cars made it through the first two turns of the last lap cleanly. But at turn 3, Kyle Busch spun out, taking 16 other cars with him. One even crossed the finish line upside down!

But the real excitement came seconds *before* the crash. Kevin Harvick and Mark Martin were racing side by side for the checkered flag when Busch spun out behind them. When the final flag waved, it was Harvick ahead of Martin by the slimmest margin since the first Daytona 500, just 0.02 second!

"This has to be the wildest Daytona 500 I've ever watched," marveled car owner Richard Childress.

The following February marked the 50th running of the Great American Race. The lead changed 17 times, with veteran driver Tony Stewart capturing first with just one lap to go. But then Stewart made a rookie mistake. He dropped to the inside to block Kyle Busch. That left space for Ryan Newman to scoot ahead. Moments later, Newman zoomed over the finish line—with Busch right behind him! Instead of first, Stewart ended up in third.

Bumping and blocking are a big part of NASCAR races, but in the 2009 Daytona 500, Brian Vickers and Dale Earnhardt Jr. used the tactics a little too aggressively. In lap 77, Vickers cut off Earnhardt, who was driving down low. Earnhardt retaliated by turning up and nudging Vickers into the pack. Ten cars were wiped out in the crash that followed. Vickers was furious, positive that Earnhardt had turned into him on purpose.

Rain cut that race short by 48 laps. That was fine with Matt Kenseth. He'd just edged into the lead when officials called an end to the day.

The red flag is usually flown to stop cars after wrecks. In 2010, it flew to stop cars because the track itself was a wreck. Pothole repairs caused long delays. So did late-race crashes that resulted in two green-white-checkered finishes! When the second checkered flag finally waved, more than six hours had passed, making it the longest race in Daytona history.

After a total of 52 lead changes, the winner was Jamie McMurray, who held off Dale Earnhardt Jr. in a last dash to the line.

"Oh, I'm going to cry!" McMurray said as he rolled into Victory Lane.

McMurray, like most race car drivers, is tough—one has to be to compete in something as dangerous as car racing. But when the distance is over and your car is first, crying with joy just somehow seems right!

★ CONCLUSION ★

The Races Continue

Car racing has been part of the American lifestyle for more than a century. Each year, hundreds of thousands of spectators crowd into venues around the country to watch their favorite drivers compete. While the Indianapolis 500 and the Daytona 500 are the most popular events, fans can take in the action in any number of smaller but equally intense races in every region of the country.

But if sitting behind the wheel rather than in the grandstands is how you want to experience car racing, then you're in luck. Kids as young as seven can learn how to race in go-karts—with a parent's permission and proper instruction, and under tight safety regulations, of course! Midget cars are another stepping-stone to the big time. Many star drivers got their starts in these small but powerful vehicles before heading for careers in open-wheeled and stock car racing. There are even summer camps that teach young people the ins and outs of driving on tracks.

To be a successful driver, it's important to know how cars work. You can take courses in auto mechanics to learn about engines or study physics to understand how and why cars behave differently under different circumstances. For instance, did you know that stock car drivers rely heavily on drafting—a maneuver in which a driver camps on another driver's bumper to reduce the drag on his car—but open-wheeled racers typically don't draft at all? That's because the air behind the skinnier open-wheeled racer is more turbulent and therefore more likely to cause a crash than help the trailing driver.

Young people can learn about car racing through websites, television, and, of course, books like this one. Lucky kids who live near speedways might be able to talk to the drivers and mechanics themselves, so long as those men and women aren't focusing on a race. No doubt they'll be the first to tell you that the best racers combine knowledge, safety, and experience into a recipe for success. So if you're ready to follow their lead, then, as the saying goes, "Start your engines!"

★ GLOSSARY ★

CRASH COURSE IN AUTO RACING

Types of Competitive Car Racing

Formula 1 (F1): Formula refers to the set of rules governing the power, size, speed, and weight of the competing cars. There are many levels within Formula racing; Formula 1 is the highest. Drivers who compete in Formula 1 events are the very best. Formula 1 races are held on roads built just for this purpose or on street circuits, not ovals.

Go-kart: Small but powerful four-wheeled vehicles that can reach speeds of 160 miles per hour. Go-kart racing is typically the first real step toward professional open-wheeled racing.

Midget cars: Midgets are larger and heavier than go-karts but are not full-size single-seater cars. Midget racing is midway up the ladder to both open-wheeled and stock car racing. Many famous drivers had their starts in midgets.

Sports car racing: Also known as grand tourers, or GTs, these cars resemble production sports cars on the outside while the inner workings are built for racing. They race on closed-circuit courses.

Touring car racing: Similar to NASCAR cars, these production models are greatly modified for racing. Events are held on road courses.

Types of Race Courses

Oval: These closed-circuit tracks have only one direction of turn (usually left). Turns are usually banked. Ovals are built specifically for racing cars. Short tracks are less than a mile long. Speedways are between one and two miles long. Super-speedways are more than two miles long. Speedway surfaces include concrete, asphalt, and dirt.

Road course: Like ovals, road courses are paved closed circuits built just for motor racing. Unlike ovals, they twist and turn in different directions. Formula 1 events take place in such venues.

Street circuit: As the name implies, these courses are made up of streets that have been temporarily closed to the public. Races must get government approval before being held; otherwise, they are illegal.

Sanctioning Bodies of Car Racing

American Automobile Association (AAA): This organization oversaw open-wheeled racing in the United States from 1905 to 1956, when it switched its focus from professional racing to member services.

United States Automobile Club (USAC): This association took over the sanctioning of open-wheeled racing from the AAA in 1956. It relinquished control in 1978, when car drivers and owners formed their own league.

Championship Auto Racing Teams (CART): In 1978, many open-wheeled car drivers and owners broke away from the USAC to form a separate league. CART promoted and protected its members and increased the sport's popularity but was later overshadowed by a new racing association.

Indy Racing League (IRL): The current open-wheeled sanctioning was formed in 1994 by Tony George (grandson of longtime Indianapolis Motor Speedway owner Tony Hulman), who felt CART had too much control over open-wheeled racing. The IRL took over all of CART in 2008. Today, it oversees three Indy car series, one of which includes the Indianapolis 500.

National Association of Stock Car Auto Racing (NASCAR): The brainchild of William France in 1948, this governing body turned stock car racing into one of the most popular spectator sports in America.

MATT CHRISTOPHER®

THE #1
SPORTS SERIES
FOR KIDS

Read them all!

*Previously published as *Crackerjack Halfback*

All available in paperback from Little, Brown and Company
**Previously published as *Baseball Pals*

Matt Christopher®

Muhammad Ali

Kobe Bryant

Dale Earnhardt Sr.

Jeff Gordon

Tony Hawk

Dwight Howard

LeBron James

Derek Jeter

Michael Jordan

Peyton and Eli Manning

Shaquille O'Neal

Albert Pujols

Jackie Robinson

Alex Rodriguez

Babe Ruth

Tiger Woods